PAINTING
watercolor *flowers*
that glow

JAN KUNZ

NORTH LIGHT BOOKS
CINCINNATI, OHIO
www.artistsnetwork.com

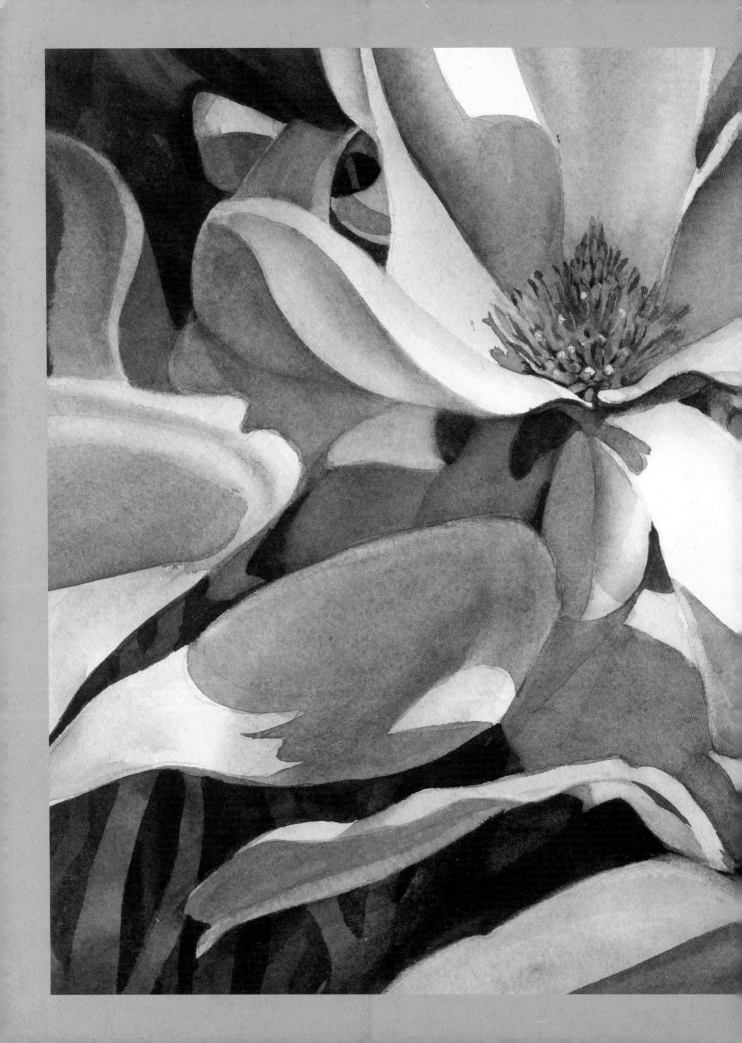

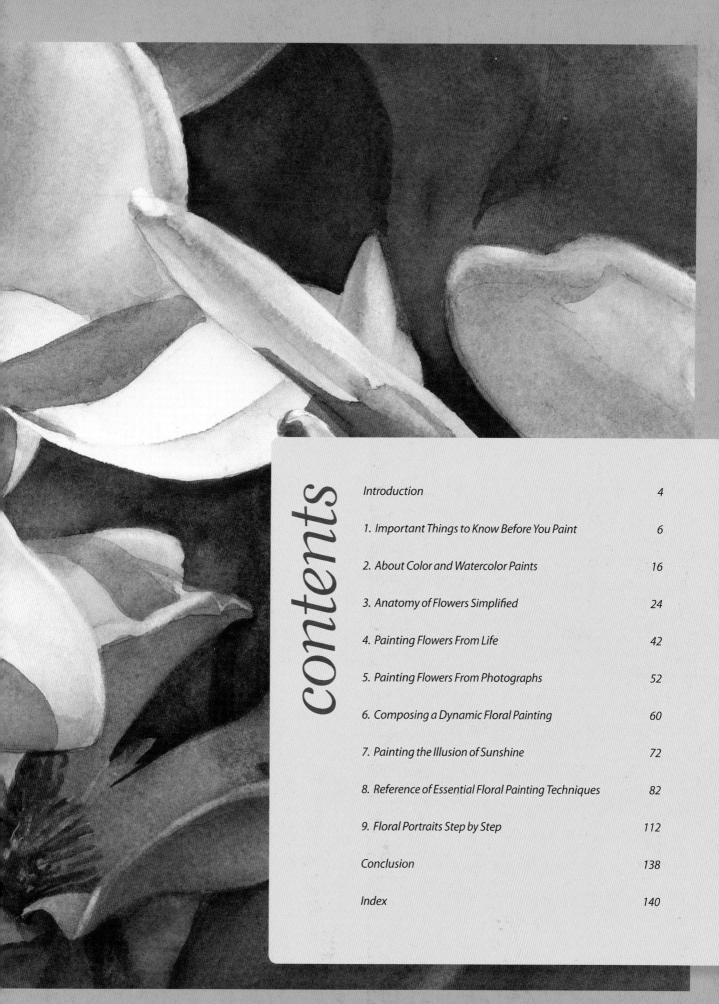

contents

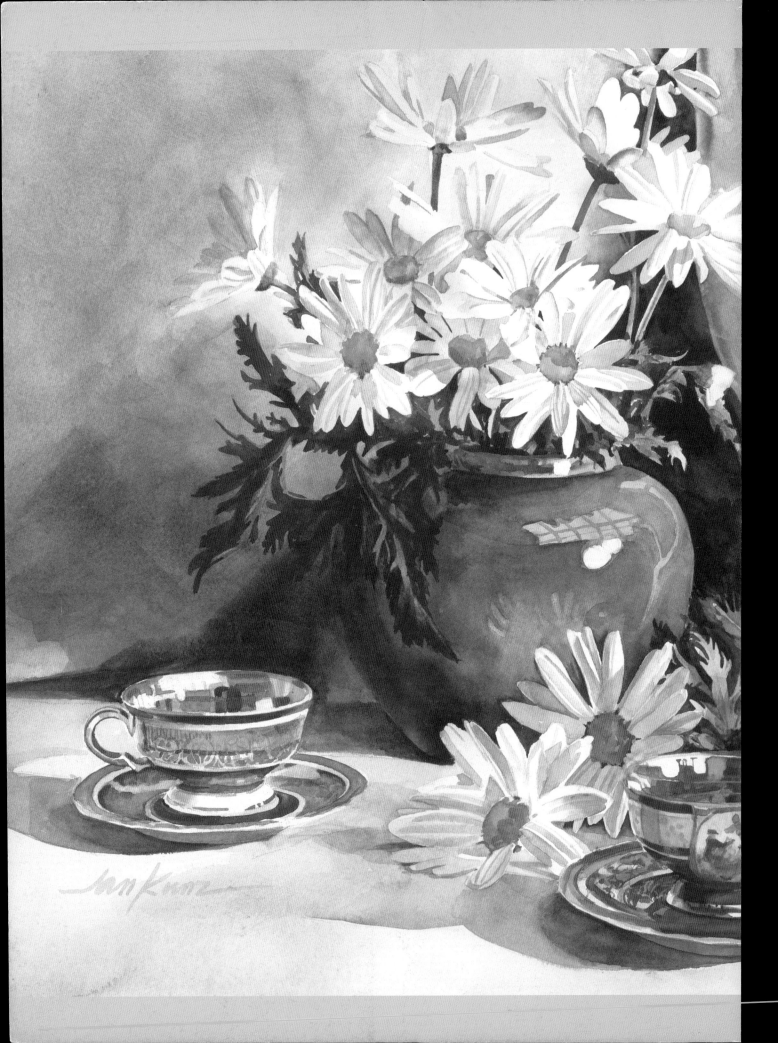

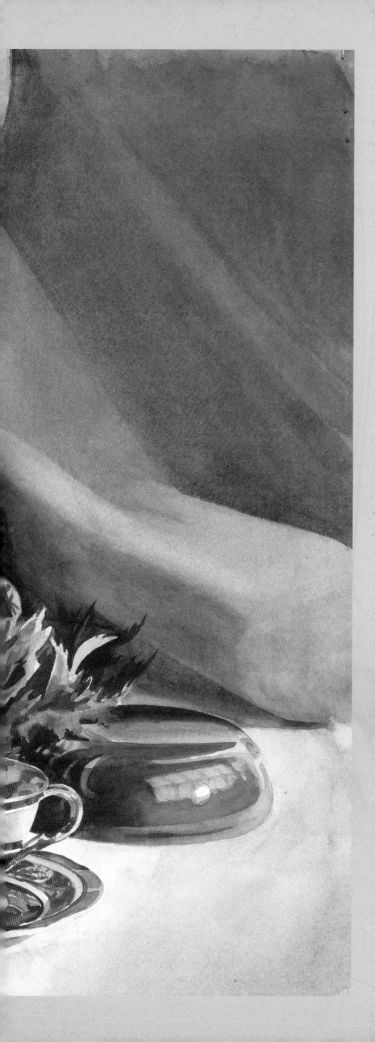

Introduction

Watercolor is great fun. Anything that will hold still long enough is liable to become the subject for a watercolor painting. Flowers are an almost perfect subject. They're incredibly beautiful, they stay quietly where you put them for a long period of time, and they don't offer suggestions or comment on your painting skill. You can paint beautiful florals even if you don't know a peony from a petunia.

That's the good news. Even better is the news that learning to really see the intricate forms and colors of the most simple blossoms will enhance your ability to see (and paint) everything!

Of course, it's not all a garden of roses. Painting flowers takes patience and concentration. You probably won't find the time to solve world problems, and now and then, you may even forget lunch!

I wish I could tell you there is a simple "one-two-three" method for painting flowers. As far as I know, there isn't one. Each new variety or floral arrangement presents a new challenge. Happily, there are a few constants. Flowers have similar folds, ruffles, convex and concave shapes. So, if you learn to paint a rounded surface on a lily, you can paint a rounded surface on a rose or any other flower. The colors may vary, but the technique is the same. For that reason I have included a section in this book describing how to paint many of the recurring shapes you'll encounter when painting flowers.

I know from experience that there are many of us who read the caption under the pictures and immediately begin to paint. However, those little paragraphs just won't hold all the information, so I hope you will read further. This book is filled with the basic techniques I have learned after years of painting for pleasure (and now and then for profit)!

There's a great deal of excitement ahead, so turn off your cell phone and let's get started.

Jan Kunz

Daisies
14½" × 18" (37cm × 46cm)

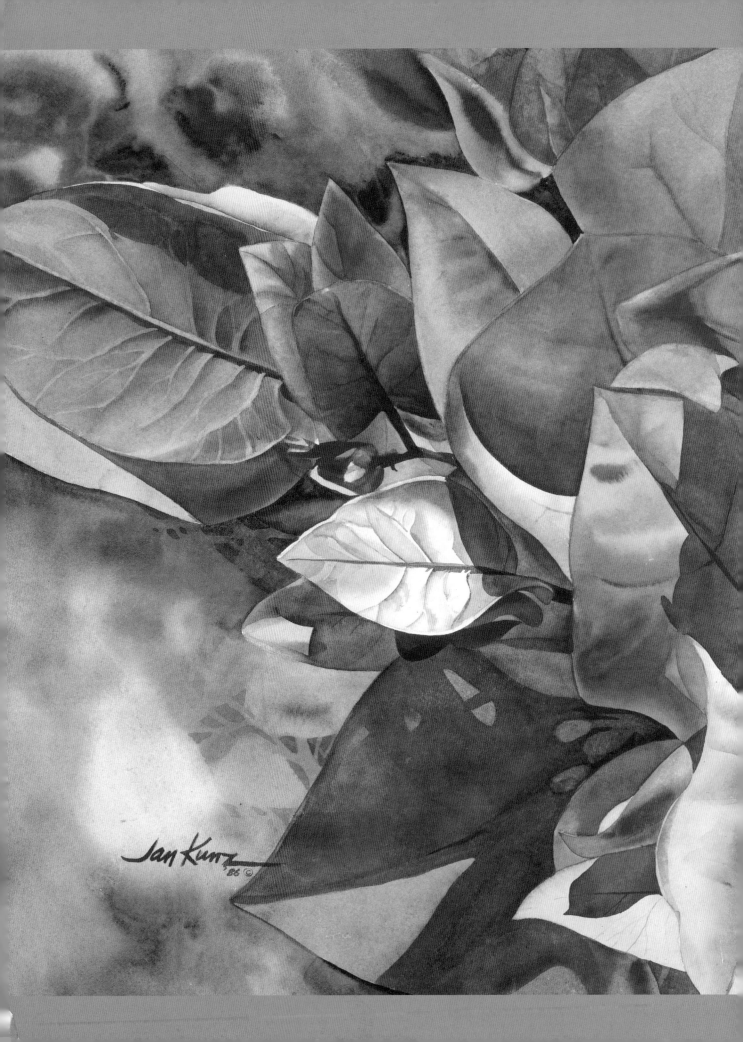

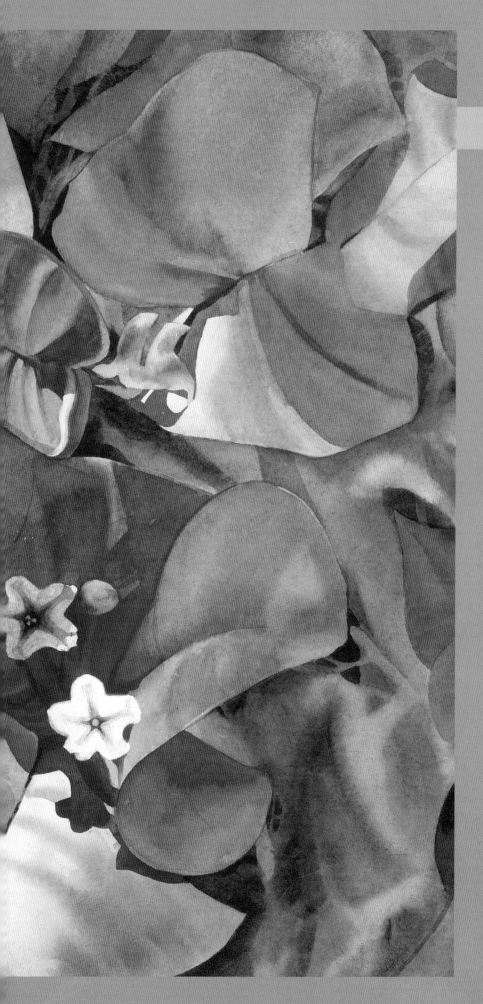

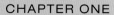

1

Important Things to Know Before You Paint

You learn to paint by painting, and it takes time and determination to become a fine painter. You may have heard that watercolor is difficult to handle, but with practice you will soon learn to control this beautiful medium and witness magical things happening before you.

Of course you will have bad days. Even experienced watercolorists struggle with bouts of frustration and self-doubt. So if you have a problem, be kind to yourself. You are becoming an artist. No one is born with a full-fledged art gene.

Here are a few things to remember:
- Don't compare yourself with other painters. You will never see their failures.
- Try to paint when you are rested and have the time.
- Don't let frustration keep you from painting.
- Celebrate your victories and learn from your failures.

Bougainvilleas
22" × 30" (56cm × 76cm)

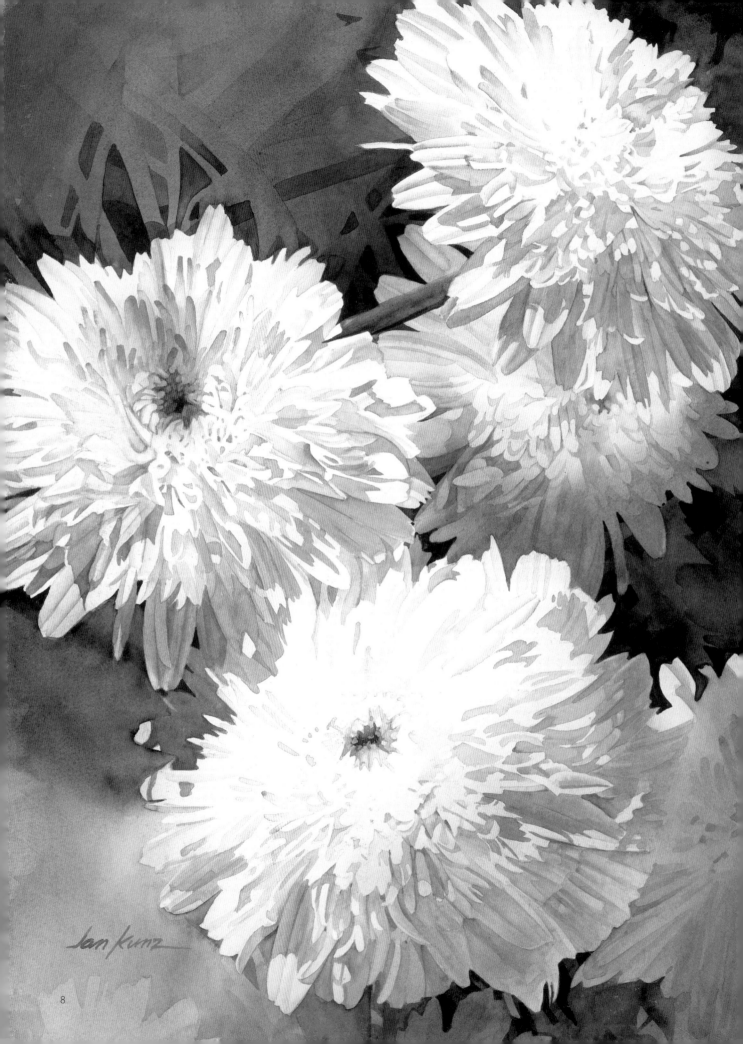

Tool Checklist

SURFACE
☐ Arches cold-press watercolor paper

WATERCOLORS
☐ Cadmium Red

☐ Cadmium Red Dark

☐ Rose Madder (Genuine)

☐ Winsor Red

☐ Burnt Umber

☐ Burnt Sienna

☐ Raw Umber

☐ Raw Sienna

☐ Cadmium Orange

☐ New Gamboge

☐ Cadmium Yellow

☐ Cerulean Blue

☐ Cobalt Blue

☐ Winsor Blue

☐ Winsor Green

☐ Sap Green

BRUSHES
☐ 1½ inch (38mm) flat brush

☐ 1 inch (25mm) flat brush

☐ Nos. 4, 6, 8, 10, 12, 14 and 24 rounds

OTHER
☐ Drawing board

☐ Sketchbook

☐ 2B drawing pencil

☐ 6B graphite stick

☐ Mat corners

☐ Frosted acetate

☐ Tracing paper

☐ Craft knife

☐ Container for water

☐ Paint rag

☐ Stapler

Most watercolor books have a section to help you select the tools and materials the author recommends. If you have as many books as I do, you are already supplied. This section is aimed at the painter who is new to watercolor and needs to get outfitted.

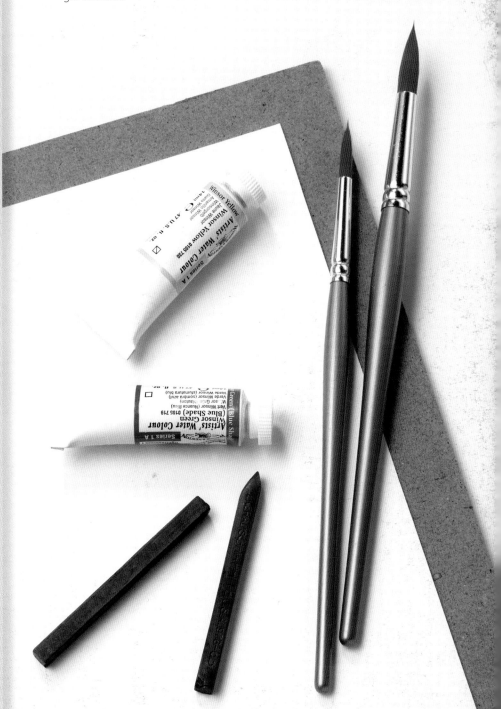

Brushes and Tools

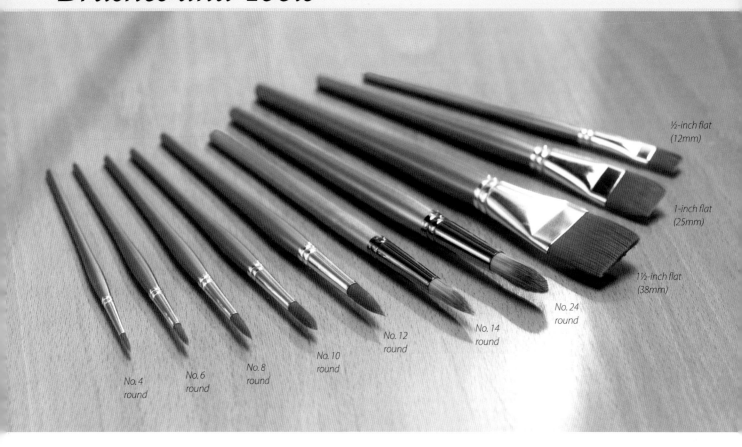

½-inch flat (12mm)

1-inch flat (25mm)

1½-inch flat (38mm)

No. 24 round

No. 14 round

No. 12 round

No. 10 round

No. 8 round

No. 6 round

No. 4 round

Brushes

There was a time when the only good brushes were made of sable hair and were very expensive! Happily, that has changed, and there are many good synthetic brands on the market.

Select a brush that holds a good quantity of water and springs back into shape after each stroke. Most good art supply dealers will supply you with a cup of water with which to test a brush before purchase.

The size brush you choose should fit the job it is intended for. Just as you wouldn't paint a house with a trim brush, you shouldn't try to run a wash with a tiny brush or paint petals with a mop!

You don't need to have all of the brushes pictured. If you have nos. 4, 8 and 14 rounds and a 1-inch (25mm) flat brush, you'll get along very well.

Modified Oil Brushes

There will be times when you will want to scrub out an offensive spot, lift a highlight or soften an edge. That is where modified oil brushes come in handy. Perhaps you can persuade an oil-painter friend to donate a couple of old bristle brushes to the cause.

I have modified two oil brushes for special use. The first is a flat no. 6 bristle brush I use along with a piece of acetate to lift highlights and make corrections. The tip of this brush is cut shorter to enhance its stiffness. The second brush is a no. 2 round bristle brush. I cut the tip of this brush at an angle to form a point, creating a great tool with which to lift small highlights.

I used to go to some trouble to modify brushes by wedging the bristles between heavy paper and cutting their tips with a utility knife. Since that time, I discovered it works just as well to wrap the bristles tightly

BRUSH SELECTION

These are my brushes in the sizes I use most often. I'll admit they have a few years on them, but a good brush can be a good friend for a long time.

with masking tape, and then cut them with scissors (or a craft knife) right through the masking tape. The tape will come off easily after the surgery.

You can create a useful tool for drawing on damp paper by sharpening the handle of one of these brushes in a pencil sharpener.

One other oil brush (not pictured) that I find useful is a flat no. 2 Grumbacher Erminette. It is small, only about ⅛-inch (3mm) wide, and I use it to soften edges. This little brush is not too stiff and is very maneuverable.

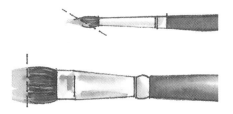

MODIFIED OIL BRUSHES
To modify these brushes for lifting highlights and making corrections, trim the tips along the dotted lines. Wrap the tip of an oil brush with masking tape and trim it with scissors.

Palette

The selection of a palette is largely a matter of personal choice, but it should have deep wells to hold the paint and large areas for mixing. I prefer a baked enamel palette. It does not stain readily, and my palette fits easily under the faucet for cleaning. I use a large 16" × 11¼" (41cm × 29cm) butcher tray for mixing big washes.

Pencils

In order to make graphite transfer paper you will need a 4B or 6B graphite stick or one of those pencils that is entirely graphite, such as a Pentalic Woodless Pencil. For sketching in the field, I usually use an HB and a 4B. For preparing the drawing in the studio, I prefer an ordinary no. 2. Too hard a pencil scars the paper, and a soft one makes a thick line and dirties both the paper and your hand.

Paint Rag

There is nothing like a good paint rag! You will hear that sponges, toilet paper or paper towels are just great, but here is one place I totally disagree! Sponges may pick up water from the brush, but they do little to wipe it clean when you want to dip into another color. Toilet paper gets soft and shredded and wets the table, and a paper towel is never where you need it. I prefer terry cloth bar towels. They are about 14" (36cm) to 16" (41cm) square; you can buy them from a restaurant supply house or by the pound from a laundry after they are too old for commercial use. You can also find them in discount grocery or department stores. An old bath towel is another option. These towels are rugged and clean up easily in the washing machine.

I begin each painting with a clean rag placed on my drawing table next to my palette. Often two or three clean rags are used during the course of one painting.

Facial Tissues

It is difficult to paint without facial tissues. You need them to wipe out the palette, pick up a spill or remove a misplaced color.

Knife

An craft knife or razor blade is a useful tool to make an acetate frisket or pick out a highlight.

Liquid Frisket

Liquid frisket is used to mask areas you want to protect when applying washes of color. I use it sparingly because the edges appear hard after it is removed. However, there are times when painting around objects is simply impractical, and nothing else will do as well.

Liquid frisket is sold at most art stores. Winsor & Newton calls theirs Art Masking Fluid, and Grumbacher's brand is Misket. Liquid frisket can ruin your brush if you aren't careful to use it according to the directions on the bottle.

Acetate Frisket

You can make an *acetate frisket* for use in lifting color from small areas. Just place the acetate over the painting and use a pencil to outline the area to be lifted. Remove the acetate and carefully cut out the outlined shape with a craft knife. Next, re-place the acetate frisket over the painting and remove the offending area with a moistened stiff brush (like the modified oil brush). Corrections of this kind nearly defy detection, but they should be used only when the painting is near completion. Stiff brushing can distress the paper to the point that it will not accept more pigment well.

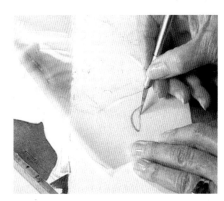

HOW TO MAKE ACETATE FRISKET
Place frosted acetate over the painting and outline the area you wish to lift. Cut out the shape you have outlined and replace the acetate over the painting and remove the offending area with a damp, stiff brush.

Surfaces

Beautiful handmade paper is a watercolorists' most important surface. In this book we use cold-pressed paper that is relatively smooth and a good surface for almost any painting technique, but there are different textured papers.

Other surfaces include sketch paper, tracing paper and acetate. These surfaces are used for drawing, planning and numerous other reasons. Acetate is transparent and can be used for drawing or for making friskets. Tracing paper can be made into graphite transfer sheets that, with proper care, will last for years.

Watercolor Paper

Many watercolor instructors urge beginning painters to work on good-quality watercolor paper and I agree. If all you want to do is practice brushstrokes, why not use old newspaper want ads? Even experienced watercolorists have real problems with poor, unwieldy paper.

What is a good watercolor paper? If you don't know how to judge good paper, start with a brand name that is recognized by artists as being top quality. The best paper is 100 percent rag, hand- or mold-made. Some of the top brands include Arches, Holbein, Fabriano, Winsor & Newton, and Strathmore watercolor board.

Most papers come in three surfaces: *hot press* (smooth), *cold press* (medium) and *rough*. In addition, watercolor paper comes in various weights. The most popular are 140-lb. (300gsm) and 300-lb. (640gsm) (The weight refers to the weight of 500 sheets.) A standard size sheet is 22" × 30" (56cm × 76cm). You can also purchase larger (elephant-size) sheets, or buy it by the roll. For the demonstrations in the book, I used 140-lb. (300gsm) or 300-lb. (640gsm) Arches cold-pressed paper.

Stretching Paper

Stretching paper prevents it from buckling once water is applied. If you use 140-lb. (300gsm) paper, I recommend that you stretch it. There's enough to think about while you are painting without worrying about wrinkled paper. Stretching isn't required for 300-lb. (640gsm) paper.

Stretching paper is easy. Have everything ready beforehand because you don't want the paper to begin to dry while you are working with it. You will need a drawing board slightly larger than the paper. Basswood, foamcore or gator board all work well. You will also need a filled staple gun. I use a regular desk stapler, but if your board is extremely hard, you may need a heavier industrial type.

Fill a large container with cool water. You can use a sink or bathtub. Place the paper into the water. If it doesn't fit, make it into a soft roll. After about two to five minutes (and when you are sure the entire paper is thoroughly wet), remove the paper and place it down flat onto your drawing board. Immediately begin to staple all around the edge, placing a staple about every two to four inches (5cm to 10cm). Paper exerts a great deal of pull as it dries, so be sure the staples are well in place. I roll a clean terry cloth towel over the surface of the paper to pick up excess water and speed drying. It is necessary that you lay the drawing board on a horizontal surface to dry. You don't want the water to run to one side and cause a buckle.

HOW TO STRETCH PAPER

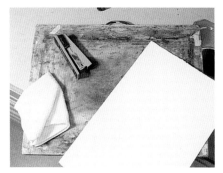

Have your paper, drawing board and filled staple gun ready before you begin.

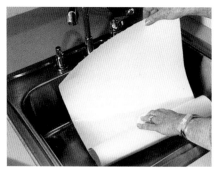

If your paper is too large to fit into the sink, make it into a soft roll and gently submerge it. Be careful not to fold or scar the paper. Hold it under water until every part is thoroughly wet.

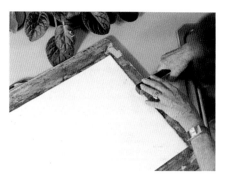

Remove the paper and lay it on your drawing board. Immediately staple opposite sides of the paper. Continue around the entire board, placing staples two to four inches (5cm to 10cm) apart.

Frosted Acetate

Frosted, or matte, acetate (depending on the brand name) sheets are translucent, and the surface readily accepts pen or pencil. The acetate sheets should be thick enough to withstand handling (0.005 or 0.007 is best). The brands I use are Grafix acetate or Pro Art. These come in a tablet of 9" × 12" (23cm × 30cm) sheets. Be sure you don't buy clear acetate—it's too smooth to accept the pencil.

You will find many uses for frosted acetate. Its nearly transparent quality makes it possible to draw on several pieces and then superimpose them on one another to create a composition.

Transfer Paper

Flowers have many complicated shapes, so I like to do my planning on tracing paper, as you will soon see. Once I am satisfied with the drawing, I transfer it onto the watercolor paper. I have never found a commercial transfer paper I like as well as the graphite one I make myself.

To make graphite transfer paper, you need a piece of good-quality tracing paper cut to almost any size. Make it large enough so you can use it again and again with various size drawings. Mine is about 18" (46cm) square.

Rub one side of the paper with a soft graphite stick or woodless pencil until it is pretty well covered. A crisscross motion works very well. Once this is accomplished, dampen a piece of facial tissue with lighter fluid or rubber cement thinner, and using a circular motion, rub over the blackened surface. The graphite will smear at first, but keep rubbing until the surface takes on a more or less uniform value. When the transfer paper is finished, I sometimes bind the edges with Scotch tape to keep the paper from tearing after repeated use.

Before you use your new transfer paper, be sure you have shaken or dusted all the excess graphite from the surface to prevent it from soiling your watercolor paper.

Use it just as you would any other paper. Put it beneath your drawing graphite side down, and trace your drawing onto the watercolor paper.

MAKE YOUR OWN TRANSFER PAPER

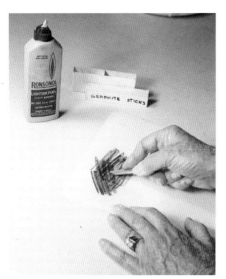

With a graphite stick or soft lead pencil, scribble lines back and forth onto a piece of good-quality tracing paper.

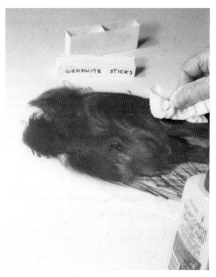

Use a piece of facial tissue moistened with lighter fluid or rubber cement thinner to rub the lines together.

Choosing Colors

In this book we will be working with transparent watercolors. The pigments that come in tubes are easiest to work with. You can squeeze out a fresh amount when you begin a painting, and the soft consistency makes it easy to use.

Many people consider all water-based paint to be watercolor, including acrylic, tempera or gouache. Be careful to get *transparent watercolor*. The label will read something like "watercolor artists' quality,"

"artists' watercolour" or "professional artists' watercolor," depending on the brand.

There are many good brands of watercolor pigments. The well-known names include Winsor & Newton, Grumbacher, Holbein and Liquitex. The color may vary slightly between different brands, but the quality remains consistently high.

How the pigments are arranged on your palette will vary. My rectangular palette has warm colors on one side and cool on the

other side. If you are happy with the way your palette is arranged, stay with it. The arrangement isn't nearly as important as knowing where a pigment is located. You don't want to stop and look around the palette for a special color while the wash is drying!

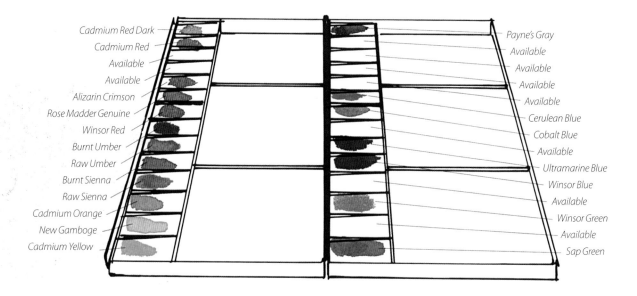

Cadmium Red Dark
Cadmium Red
Available
Available
Alizarin Crimson
Rose Madder Genuine
Winsor Red
Burnt Umber
Raw Umber
Burnt Sienna
Raw Sienna
Cadmium Orange
New Gamboge
Cadmium Yellow

Payne's Gray
Available
Available
Available
Available
Cerulean Blue
Cobalt Blue
Available
Ultramarine Blue
Winsor Blue
Available
Winsor Green
Available
Sap Green

MY PALETTE COLORS
The available spaces are used when I want to add a special color for a particular painting, such as Rose Dore, Quinacridone Gold, Phthalo Red, Winsor Violet or Cobalt Violet, or Hooker's Green Deep, Prussian Blue, Antwerp Blue or Manganese Blue. I do not own a tube of black pigment.

Painting Tips

You can't have painted as long as I have and not come up with some definite opinions. So, at the expense of sounding like your mother, here is some advice.

Stay Organized

It may seem like a trivial thing, but a well-organized work space can help you work more efficiently. When painting, your entire concentration should be on the painting itself. By the time you put brush to paper, everything else should be in order. A clean paint rag should be positioned next to your palette for immediate use. The water bucket should be large and full of clean water. All the brushes you might need should be placed for easy access (I use a jar or carousel), and facial tissue should be within reach.

Clean Your Palette and Paint

Palettes get dirty, so most of us wipe them out frequently. When cleaning your palette, don't overlook the pigment. Color is transferred from pigment to pigment during the painting process, and colors can lose their brilliance. I like to take my palette to the sink and run a gentle stream of cool water directly onto the pigments. Then, using one of my small brushes, I gently remove

any color that doesn't belong. Next, I give the palette a quick shake to remove excess water and wipe it dry. I'm very careful if the pigment is fresh. Even at that, very little pigment is lost, and what is left is fresh and brilliant.

Small Cautions That Can Help

Keeping the water container filled to the top will prevent missing the water altogether. It's easier than you think to bring a dry or dirty brush to the paper! Use a clean paint rag and replace it as necessary. In my estimation, sponges, paper towels and toilet paper make poor substitutes.

Most Important Tip

Don't listen to any of this advice if it doesn't sound right for you. That goes for any other advice you may have heard. Watercolor painting is a very personal experience. You are in charge. Have faith in your own ability to know what works for you.

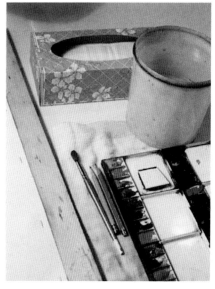

A well-organized work space can make painting easier. Your paint rag, water and facial tissue should always be within easy reach.

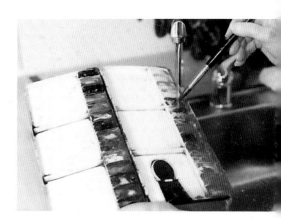

I use a gentle stream of water to clean my palette and the pigments during the painting process.

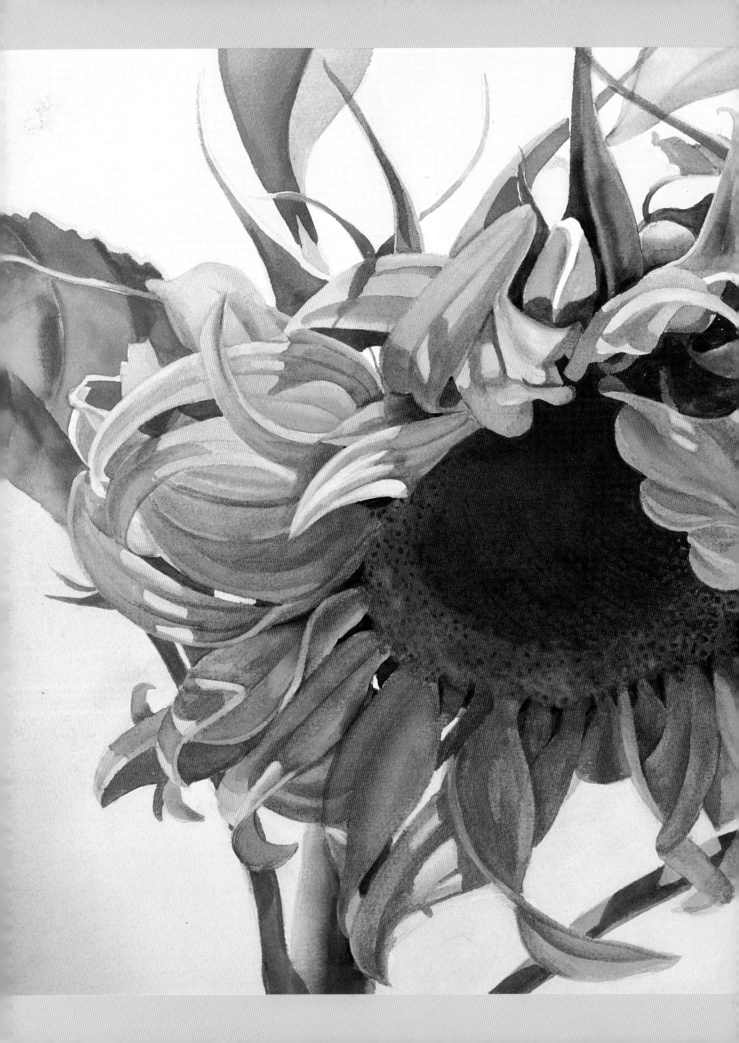

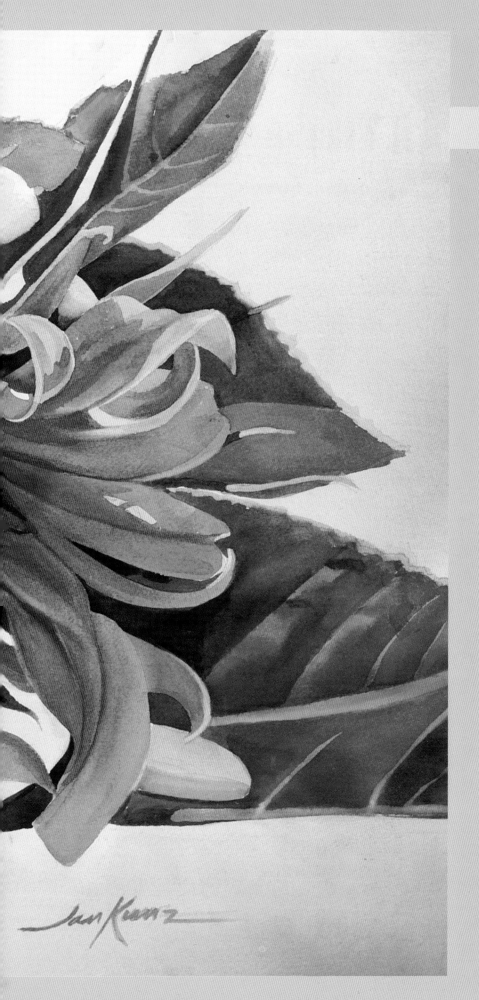

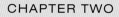

2

CHAPTER TWO

About Color and Watercolor Paints

Learning to use color effectively is highly personal and can be a lifelong pursuit. Fortunately there are many good books available on the subject and your good taste and judgment will help guide you. Names like Quinacridone Red, Naples Yellow and Perylene Maroon may seem confusing, but they simply identify the compound from which a particular pigment is made. Frequently new compounds appear on the market and I urge you to experiment with them to discover their properties. Nonetheless, it is reassuring to remember that there are only three basic hues: red, yellow and blue.

The pigments described here have been in use for many years and will be used for decades to come. Artist Ted Kautzky wrote, "With three colors we are rich." It is not how many colors you use, it is how you use them that counts.

Garden Super Star
14" × 23" (36cm × 58cm)

Color Theory

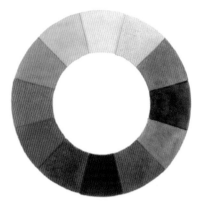

Color wheel

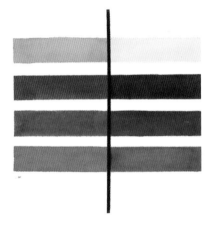

Warm and cool versions of the same hue

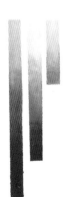

VALUE RANGE
Yellow has only a short value range. Alizarin Crimson has a very long value range. Cobalt Blue's value range is somewhere between the two.

We sense color when our eyes are struck by light waves of varying length. Our eyes pick up these waves and translate them as light. If there is no light, there is no sight, as you know if you have ever experienced total darkness.

Light and Pigment

Even though we call it "white light," the light that comes from the sun contains all the colors we see around us. Every colored object we see contains pigments that have the ability to absorb certain rays of color and reflect others. For example, a banana is yellow because the pigment in its skin reflects only the yellow light we see and absorbs all the other colors.

Through the years, some materials have been found to be especially rich in pigment. These are the materials that are purified and made into the paints we use.

Hue

Hue is the term used to name a color. Red, green, yellow and blue are hues. It has nothing to do with whether the color is intense or pale, dark or light.

Primary Colors

The *primary colors* are red, yellow and blue. These colors cannot be made with a combination of any other pigments.

Secondary Colors

Secondary colors are those colors we can make by mixing the primary hues. Each secondary is a combination of the primaries on both sides of it. Red and blue make purple. Red and yellow make orange. Blue and yellow make green. All the other colors are some mixture of the three primaries and three secondary colors.

Complementary Colors

When we place the primary and secondary colors equidistant from one another and then fill in the spaces by mixing adjacent colors, we will have created a color wheel. The colors located opposite one another are called *complementary colors*. Red and green, yellow and purple are examples of complementary colors. When complementary colors are mixed, the result is a neutral gray. Complementary colors in dark values are almost always muddy.

Warm and Cool Colors

When we speak of *warm* and *cool* colors, we are talking about color temperature, not about value or color intensity.

Many of the pigments we use in watercolor have warm and cool versions of the same color. Alizarin Crimson is a cooler red than Cadmium Red, for example.

Value

Value refers to the lightness or darkness of a color. Different pigments have different value ranges. Value range refers to the number of intermediate values you can get by using a color directly from the tube (darkest value) and then adding water until it becomes a faint tint.

Watercolor Pigments

We can assume most professional watercolor pigments are permanent and chemically stable. Certainly, they are as enduring as oil pigments. Watercolors do have unique qualities that we need to understand.

Opaque and Transparent Pigments

You don't have to work with watercolor very long to become aware that there are two kinds of watercolor pigments. Some pigments display a far degree of opacity while others are extremely transparent.

Think of opaque (or precipitating) colors as being little microscopic granules of pigment. When we paint with opaque colors, these little chunks of pigment remain deposited on the surface of the watercolor paper. When light is returned from an opaque color, it reflects only from the pigment granules.

Transparent (or staining) colors are more luminous than opaque ones. The reason is that light rays penetrate the thin film of transparent pigment and reflect the white paper beneath.

Color Sense

The selection of the color scheme and the palette we use will be largely determined by the flowers we wish to portray.

As you gain experience, you will use fewer hues, but you will take advantage of color differences that can be created by variations of color temperature, value and intensity.

It is important to give life to whatever color you use by making it "move." This means you must avoid painting a solid color and value from side to side and up and down any area if you are to avoid a poster look.

Here is some advice that I believe will serve you well. Save pure yellow for the foreground (yellow objects in the distance are yellow-green or yellow-orange). Keep the number of hues to a minimum. Remember, always put a little warm in the cool areas and a little cool in the warm areas!

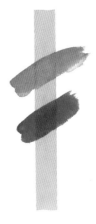

Opaque and transparent colors

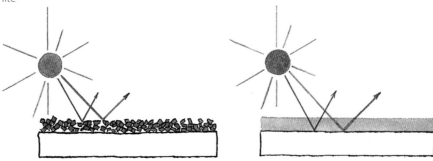

Light bounces off color granules of opaque pigments, but light reflects the white paper beneath transparent pigments.

Mixing Sparkling Darks

If ever clean, beautiful colors were important, they are important when you paint flowers!

The 40 Percent Rule

If we are to create the illusion of sunshine in our painting, we must observe the *40 percent rule*. According to this rule, the shadow side (if no reflected light is present) and the cast shadows must be a full 40 percent darker than the sunlit side. In other words, in a value scale gradated from value 1 (white) to value 10 (black), the shadow side must be a full four values darker than the sunlit side. With long-range pigment, we have nothing to worry about. For example, to paint a green box whose sunny side is value 5, use Winsor Green for both the sunny side and the shadow sides. The problem arises with colors such as yellow or orange. These are not dark enough, even right out of the tube, to paint the shadow sides of objects.

Using the Color Wheel

How can we mix a brilliant, dark value of a color with a short value range? The answer is to mix it with a color having a long value range from the same side of the color wheel.

To help you see this more clearly, I have divided the color wheel in half. This division, falling between yellow-green and yellow at the top and violet and red-violet at the bottom, separates the warm and cool colors.

The colors that are located close to one another are harmonious because each color contains some of the color lying next to it. The colors near the bottom of the color wheel are darker in value than those near the top.

Your mixtures will remain brilliant as long as you combine colors from only one side of the color wheel. Select a pigment from the opposite side and you will have mixed a gray.

It's true that many fine artists are known for using beautiful grays in their paintings. Grays can be wonderful in light and middle values. You can get into trouble, however, if you use neutral grays in dark values, especially over a large area of your painting.

Remember, mixing complementary colors in values darker than 6 equals mud!

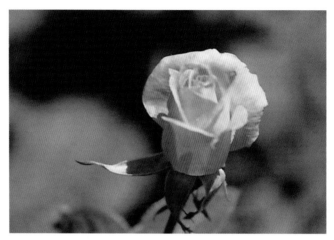

To paint high-contrast subjects in bright sunlight you will need to mix dark values of colors that have a short value range, such as yellow. You can keep these darks brilliant (avoiding mud) by mixing them with darker colors from the same side of the color wheel, rather than with a complement from the opposite side of the wheel.

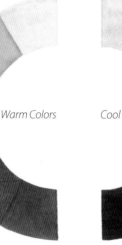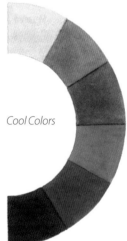

Warm Colors *Cool Colors*

Pigment Chart

Most watercolor pigments fit into one of four groups.

1. *High-intensity opaques*
2. *Low-intensity opaques*
3. *Low-intensity transparents*
4. *High-intensity transparents*

The following chart will help you compare various watercolor pigments. The notation under Similar Color Comparison (SCC) will tell you whether a pigment is warm or cool when compared to another pigment of the same hue. For example, French Ultramarine Blue's SCC notation will be W, because it is a warm blue when compared to Indigo Blue, whose SCC is C to show it is a cool blue. M indicates the color is midway between warm and cool; it is a pure hue. Some colors were left blank because I know of no comparable pigments from a tube.

Although some of the pigments in Groups 2 and 3 have very long value ranges, they will appear muddy and lifeless if used singly in dark values. Mix these colors with a long-range transparent from the same side of the color wheel.

Properties of Watercolor Pigments

Pigment	Warm/ Cool	Similar Color Comparison	Darkest Value	Opaque	Paper Staining	Transparent	Black Content
High-Intensity Opaques							
Cadmium Yellow	W	W	2+	Very	Slight	No	None
Cadmium Orange	W		3+	Very	Slight	No	None
Cadmium Red	W	W	4+	Very	Slight	No	None
Vermilion	W	W	4+	Yes	Slight	No	None
Cerulean Blue	C	C	4+	Very	Slight	No	None
Cobalt Blue	C	M	5+	Very	Slight	No	None
Low-Intensity Opaques							
Yellow Ochre	W	W	3+	Yes	Slight	No	Slight
Raw Sienna	W	W	4+	Yes	Medium	No	Slight
Raw Umber	W	C	6+	Yes	Slight	No	High
Burnt Sienna	W		6+	Partly	Medium	Slightly	Slight
Burnt Umber	W		8+	Yes	Slight	No	High
Low-Intensity Transparents							
Brown Madder (Alizarin)	W		8+	No	High	Yes	Medium
Indigo	C	C	9+	No	High	Yes	Medium
Payne's Gray	C		10+	No	Medium	Yes	Medium
Sap Green	C	W	6+	No	High	Yes	Medium
High-Intensity Transparents							
New Gamboge	W	C	2+	No	Slight	Yes	None
Winsor Red	W	M	5+	Slightly	Medium	Yes	None
Alizarin Crimson	W	C	8+	No	High	Yes	None
Winsor Blue	C	C	10+	No	High	Yes	None
Winsor Green	C	C	10+	No	High	Yes	None
French Ultramarine Blue	C	W	8+	Slightly	Nearly	No	None

GROUP 1: HIGH-INTENSITY OPAQUES

These opaque pigments have very short value ranges. They are useful for overpainting or for bright accents.

Cadmium Yellow *An opaque, warm yellow. Can be used for bright accents. Mixes well with Cadmium Red to produce a brilliant orange.*

Cadmium Orange *A pure opaque orange. I use it alone or mixed with various reds to add brilliance. Mixed with Winsor Blue or Winsor Green, the result is a rich grayed green.*

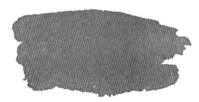

Cadmium Red *This brilliant, glowing red dries considerably lighter than you might suspect. The pigment is opaque and heavy; therefore, it can easily be moved about in a puddle of water.*

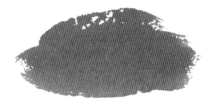

Vermilion *Vermilion is a beautiful, brilliant (toward orange) red. It is more brilliant than Cadmium Red and a good deal more expensive.*

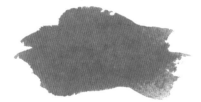

Cerulean Blue *This is a heavy, chalky pigment. Used next to Ultramarine Blue or Winsor Blue, it suggests reflected light. Next to Rose Madder, it becomes a cool accent.*

Cobalt Blue *The blue has many uses. A slightly opaque pigment, it is used to "glaze back" an overly demanding area. Combined with other pigments, it make beautiful secondary colors.*

GROUP 2: LOW-INTENSITY OPAQUES

These pigments have varying value ranges. They contain black, and used singly in dark values, tend to appear lifeless and dull.

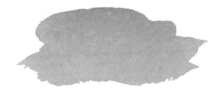

Yellow Ochre *I use Yellow Ochre very seldom. It is grayed yellow, and I find it somewhat greasy. Mixed with red, it produces a grayed orange.*

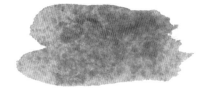

Raw Sienna *I use it with green or blue to produce a grayed green in light values. Used alone, or next to Burnt Sienna, it can suggest the edge of old leaves.*

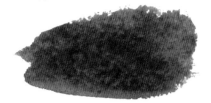

Raw Umber *This is a dark, almost greenish yellow. I like to use a touch of this color with Winsor Blue to suggest cool, grayed shadows.*

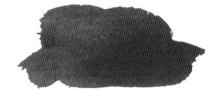

Burnt Sienna *A grayed, versatile orange that can create beautiful grays. Used alone in small areas, it suggests rust spots on flowers or burnt leaves.*

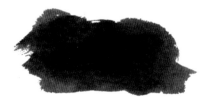

Burnt Umber *This warm brown should never be used singly in dark values, but mixed with Alizarin Crimson, it makes a wonderful near-black for crevices.*

GROUP 3: LOW-INTENSITY TRANSPARENTS

These colors have long value ranges, but like the low-intensity opaque colors, they contain black. If used alone in values darker than 6, these colors appear flat and lifeless.

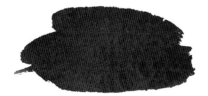

Brown Madder (Alizarin) *This is a beautiful, rich red-brown. Combined with New Gamboge, it makes a brilliant substitute for Burnt Sienna. I sometimes like to "charge" this color into other reds.*

Indigo *A blue-black "garlic" pigment—a little goes a long way. This pigment and Payne's Gray (right) have a place on my palette, but I find little use for either of them in floral painting.*

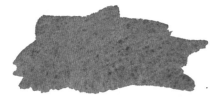

Payne's Gray *A cold gray. I try to avoid this color because it can become too convenient. Overuse can result in gray paintings.*

Sap Green *An intense (toward orange) green. I like this color combined with a Sienna for a grayed green and with Winsor Blue or Winsor Green. It is hard to handle and will stain paper, so use it with care.*

GROUP 4: HIGH-INTENSITY TRANSPARENTS

These brilliant pigments remain luminous at all value levels unlike those in group 2 and 3. They contain no black. The pigments in this group can combine with any other to achieve lively, dark values.

New Gamboge *This is a clean, brilliant yellow. (Don't confuse this color with Gamboge, which is dull by comparison.) It can be used to suggest reflected light. It mixes well to make brilliant secondaries.*

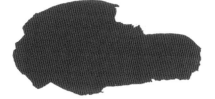

Winsor Red *This powerful red is less transparent than other pigments in this group. I use it singly or with other reds to intensify their color. Mixed with New Gamboge, it makes a brilliant orange.*

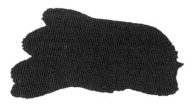

Alizarin Crimson *This cool, versatile red is my favorite. It has a very long value range and can extend the range of other pigments. Also, it mixes to make beautiful secondaries. This is probably the most-used pigment on my palette.*

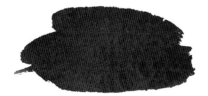

Winsor Blue *Also called Thalo or Phthalocyanine Blue, this is a cool, transparent blue. Used alone, this color tends to dominate. It's useful in mixing beautiful foliage colors.*

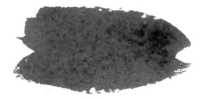

Winsor Green *An intense, cool green. Like Winsor Blue, this color can combine with others to create beautiful foliage. It's also known as Thalo or Phthalocyanine Green.*

French Ultramarine Blue *This warm blue can be considered transparent or opaque depending on how it's used. Mixed with Alizarin Crimson, it makes a wonderful violet. With Burnt Sienna, it makes a beautiful gray.*

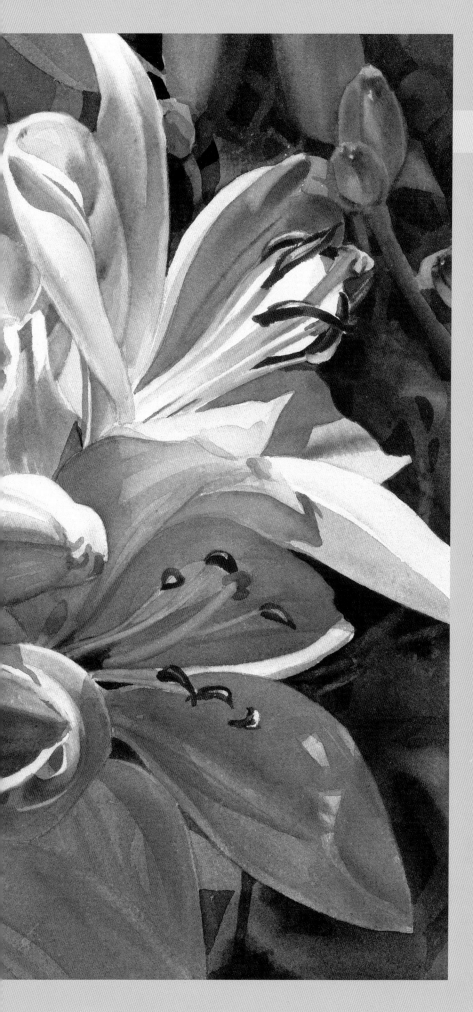

Anatomy of Flowers Simplified

Anatomy may sound like a strange word to show up in a book on floral painting. Watercolor florals are a natural subject for splash and color, but to paint them convincingly we need to know how flowers are put together and a great deal more.

The purpose of this chapter is to heighten your awareness of the form, color, texture and growth patterns of the flowers you paint. Whether your goal is a detailed portrait of flowers, or a loose interpretation of their form and brilliance, the better you know your subject, the better chance you have for a successful painting.

Oregon Gold
15" × 22" (38cm × 56cm)

Shape and Dimension

Form, or shape, is important because we humans see only shapes, values, edges and color. From an artist's point of view, a flower's anatomy is made up of basic forms.

Shape

Shape identifies the object. The chief differences between a beginner and a skilled artist are the awareness of subtle differences between shapes and the ability to transfer them to the paper. Flowers possess many shapes, and we must train ourselves to see them. Value and edges further identify objects and add detail and interest.

Dimension

Flowers, along with everything else in nature, have three dimensions. Therefore, if you want your flowers to look lifelike, you have to create the illusion of three dimensions in your paintings. Every object in the composition, including the table upon which the flowers rest and the vase in which they are placed, must look as if it has room to exist in space. It is important to create this illusion of depth.

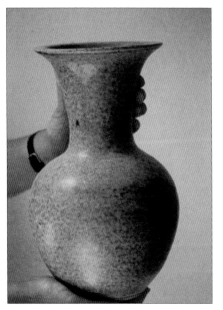

In the photograph, it takes two hands to hold the vase. It's heavy and there is no doubt it's a solid, three-dimensional form.

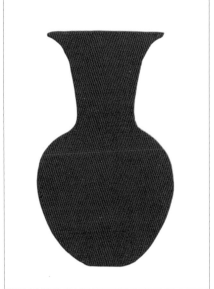

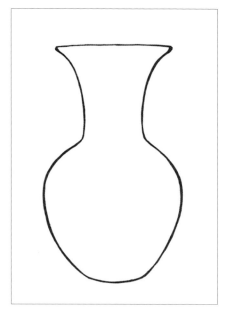

In contrast, the silhouette has the same shape as the vase, but it looks flat and is obviously not real. You would not mistake it for a real vase.

Creating the Illusion of Reality

You can see how important it is to know how to draw objects so they appear to exist in space. Probably the best way to accomplish this illusion of three-dimensional forms is to "construct" objects as you draw them. Think of all of the objects in your composition as being transparent. As you draw each object, let the lines follow around the back and the sides. In this way you can see that every element in your drawing has depth in space. Not only will you create the illusion of reality, but you will be better able to avoid the appearance of two different objects occupying the same space. You will create an illusion of a solid form in space.

Before you decide to give up painting flowers and take up something easy like brain surgery, let me assure you, constructing objects as you draw them isn't as difficult as it may seem.

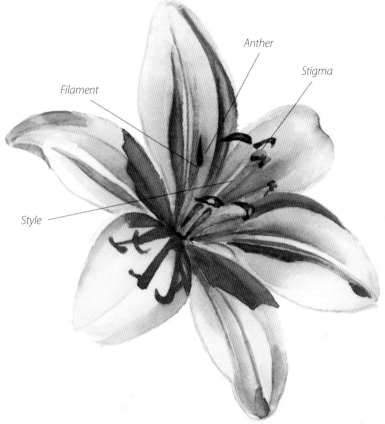

Filament

Anther

Stigma

Style

ANATOMY OF A FLOWER

Before we get to the nitty-gritty of drawing flowers, there are a few terms you should know. As you may remember from high school biology class, flower parts have names, so rather than direct you to "that little thing sticking up in the middle," here's a diagram of the flower's parts. I promise this is as technical as we will get!

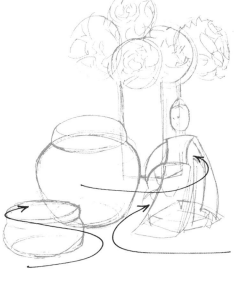

By drawing objects as if they were transparent, you can actually "construct" objects as you draw them. Doing so assures that every element in your composition has room to exist in space.

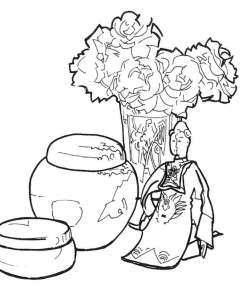

Basic Forms

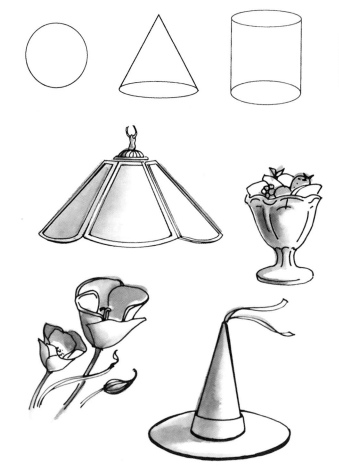

Many years ago, some intelligent artist discovered that there are four basic forms in nature. No matter how complicated an object may appear, it is basically:

- a cone
- a sphere
- a cylinder
- a cube

or some combination of these forms. You can draw anything if you can draw these simple forms.

It is true that many of the basic forms as they appear in nature aren't perfect. A banana is cylindrical in shape, but it is rather flat on the sides and turns up at the ends. An apple can be thought of as spherical, but the shape has soft edges and is somewhat elongated. Nevertheless, once you get the basic form down on paper, your drawing will be well on the way to satisfactory completion.

Try to get into the habit of recognizing the basic forms of the objects you draw before you turn your attention to any detail. Once you've identified the overall outer shapes, be sure to be equally careful with the internal shapes that describe a particular object.

In the illustrations on the following pages, I began each drawing by establishing basic form of the flower. No matter how much detail was added, the underlying structure is still visible. In paintings shown in later chapters, you will see that we can eliminate much of the detail and still create beautiful flowers as long as the basic shapes are maintained.

CONE

The cone is a favorite shape of nature. The cone (or modified cone shapes) is to be found in many flowers, mountains and even the waters of a whirlpool. The pyramids of Egypt are modified cones. Here are a few examples of familiar cone shapes.

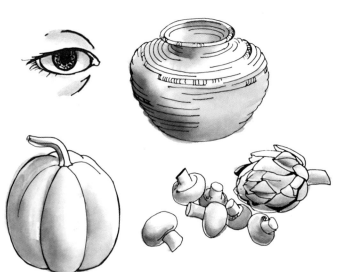

SPHERE

Half a sphere shape is the basic form for many bowls, cups and vases. The shape of many fruits and vegetables is basically spherical. I always begin drawing the human eye by first constructing a sphere.

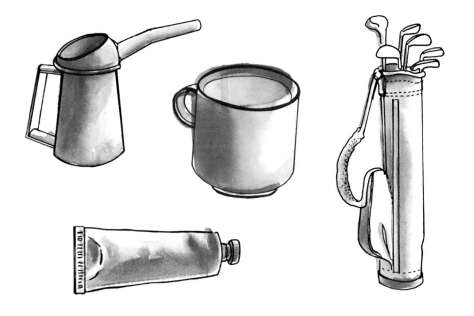

CYLINDER

Your tubes of paint, along with many vases, jars, cans and tires, are cylindrical in shape. Modified cylinders can become golf bags, paintbrushes, arms and legs. Learning to identify the basic form of an object can help make drawing easier.

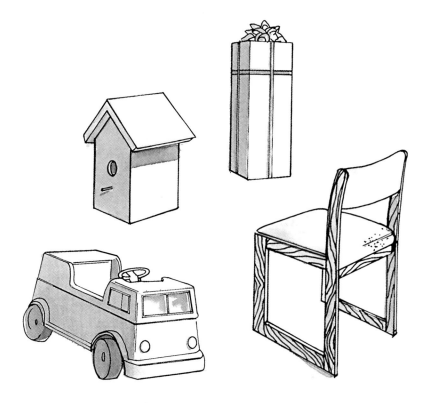

CUBE

The cube is a very familiar shape. Books, boxes, TVs, telephones, toys and many other objects are cubes or modified cubes. You are probably sitting on a cube right now.

Flowers with Simple Forms

Daisies and similar flowers are shaped like a disk or thin slice of a cylinder. Viewed straight on, these flowers are circular with petals that radiate from the center. Color, shape and size of the petals vary depending on the specimen.

Viewed from an angle, the shape is elliptical. The disk-shaped flowers in this illustration are modified to represent daisies.

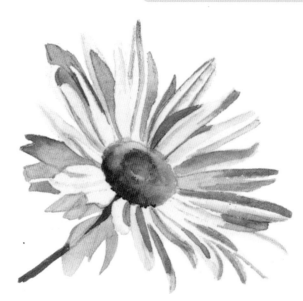

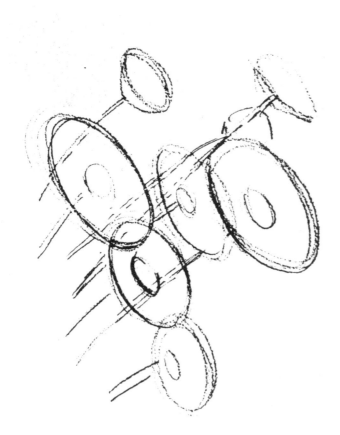

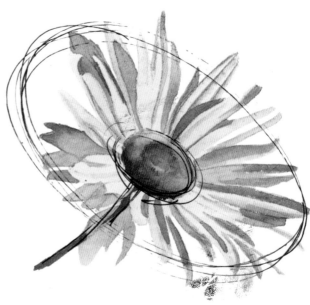

DAISIES

In laying out these sketches, I drew the forms freely. The purpose of these drawings is to plan the overall shapes, locate the stems and determine the placement of each blossom.

A daisy is formed like a disk or a thin slice of a cylinder. I use cylindrical shapes to help place the daisies. The stems are long, slender cylinders and appear to be emanating from the center of each disk shape. Notice that the partly opened blossoms are sketched as modified cones. Seeing objects as basic forms makes them easier to draw.

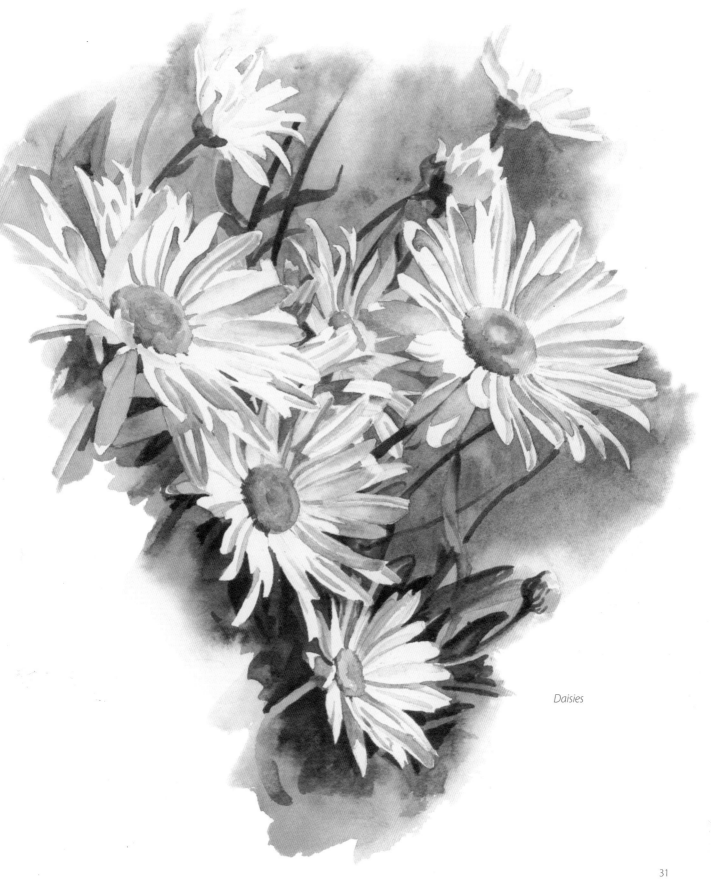

Daisies

Flowers with Simple Forms

Many flowers have spherical shapes. Thistle, roses and peonies are three examples. To paint these flowers, begin with a sphere. The particular variety of flower is of secondary importance.

In this illustration, notice that the emphasis is on the sphere shape. Sure, I had fun painting all the petals to make it look complicated. However, every brushstroke was intended to enhance the feeling of roundness.

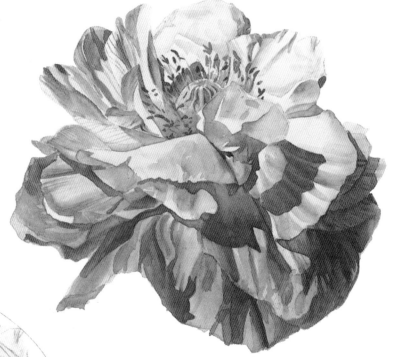

PEONIES

Peonies are sphere shaped. I swing my arm to inscribe large circles. Obviously, none of these forms are perfectly shaped, but most shapes in nature are not geometrically perfect. Nonetheless, there is a feeling of roundness.

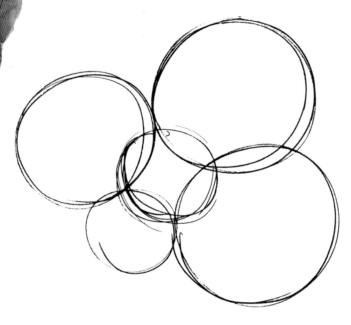

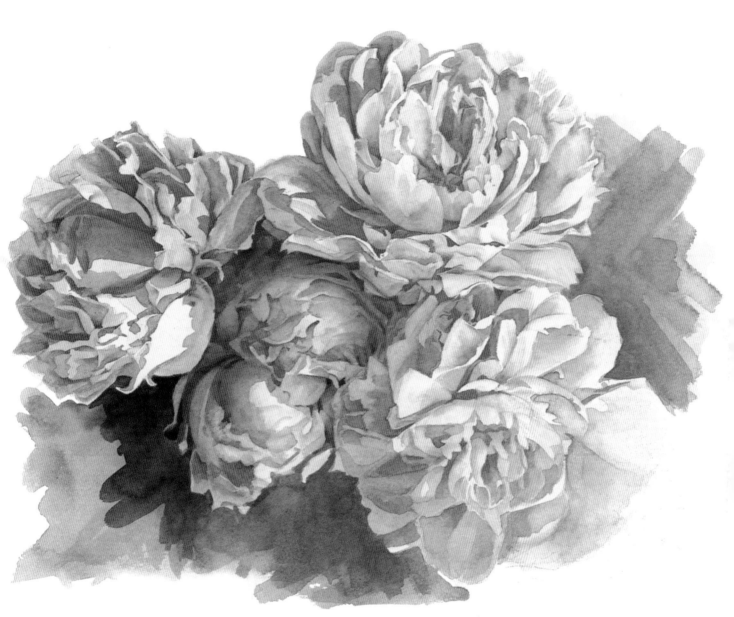

Peonies

Flowers with Simple Forms

The cone shape is very common among flowers. Lilies, fox glove, lilacs, larkspur and many others are basically shaped like a cone. Some flowers, such as rhododendrons and hyacinths have individual cone-shaped flowers, but their blooms are composed of several individuals. The collection of individual blooms forms a sphere or a cylinder.

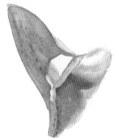

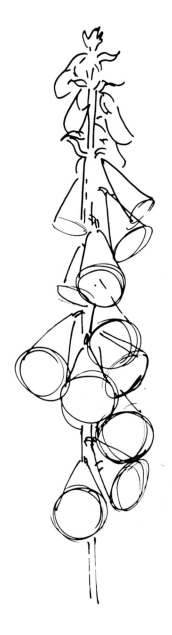

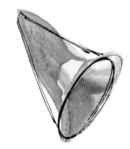

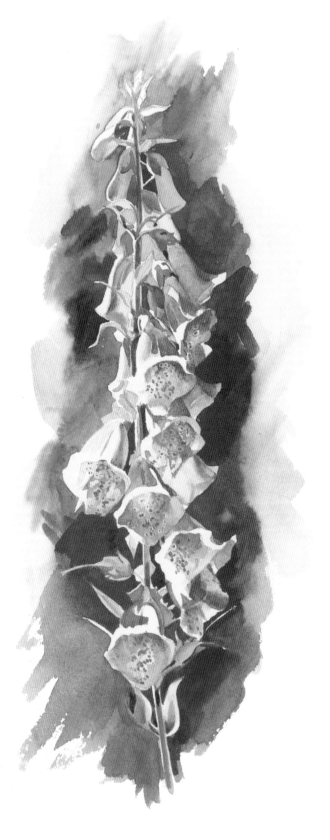

FOXGLOVE

The foxglove bloom is a collection of the bell- or cone-shaped blossoms growing on a single cylindrical stem. Once the basic form is established, it is an easy job to suggest a field of these beautiful wildflowers with simple cone shapes.

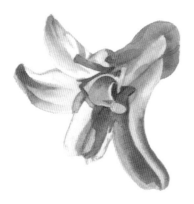
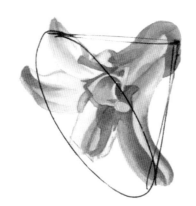
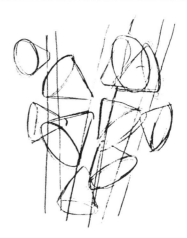

HYACINTH

This hyacinth blossom is also cone shaped, but is segmented into petals. In this worm's-eye view, the cone-shaped blossoms hang from a central stem. The sketch permits the logical overlapping of blossom shapes.

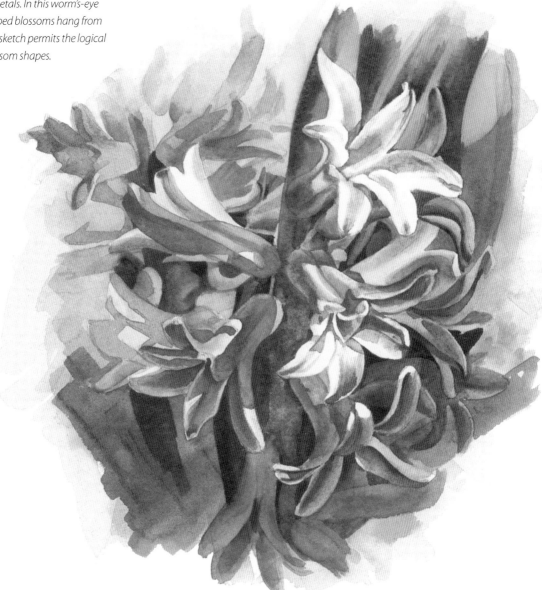

Multi-Shaped Flowers

Most flowers are made up of a combination of basic forms. Once you begin to think about basic forms, you will have little trouble recognizing them in every flower you draw. Daffodils are formed of a small cylinder occupying the center of a larger disk.

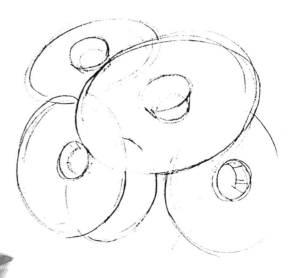

DAFFODIL

The shape of a daffodil is that of a cylinder placed on top of a disk. The base is wide and disk shaped (or a thin slice of a cylinder). The top cylinder is somewhat long but with a smaller diameter.

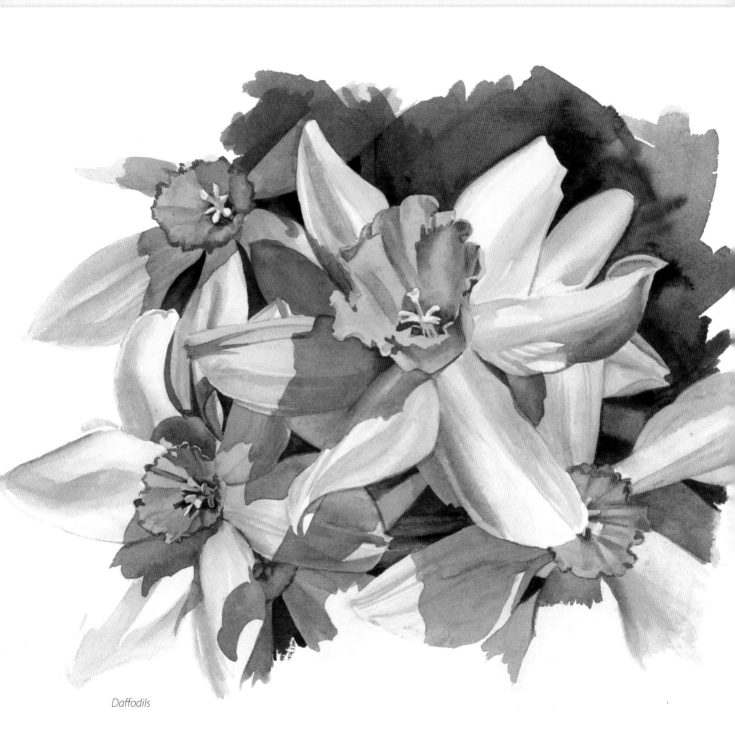

Daffodils

Multi-Shaped Flowers

Irises are also a combination of shapes. I see them as two spheres. The top portion of the flower, whose petals curl up toward the center, encases the smaller of the spheres. The larger, bottom sphere is composed of petals bending back to encircle the stem.

Now you have the idea. Think basic form. Paint any flower you choose, but think basic form first! It has been said that form drawing is fundamental to all art. Become aware of the objects you draw as solid forms having depth.

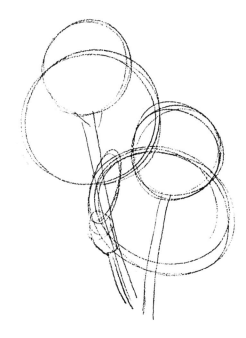

IRIS

An iris can be thought of as two spheres, one above the other. The cylindrical-shaped stem begins at the bottom of the top sphere, and the bottom sphere envelops it. The bud is ovoid shaped—like a balloon that has been squeezed into an elongated shape. The tip of the bud is located slightly behind the top flower and pushes into the petal above it. Remember to make visual space for every form in your painting.

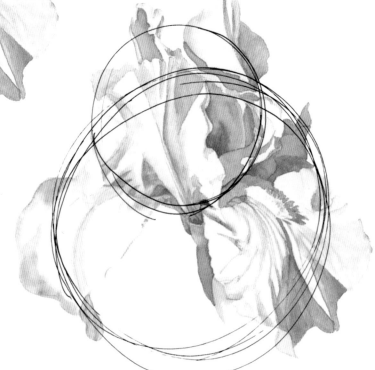

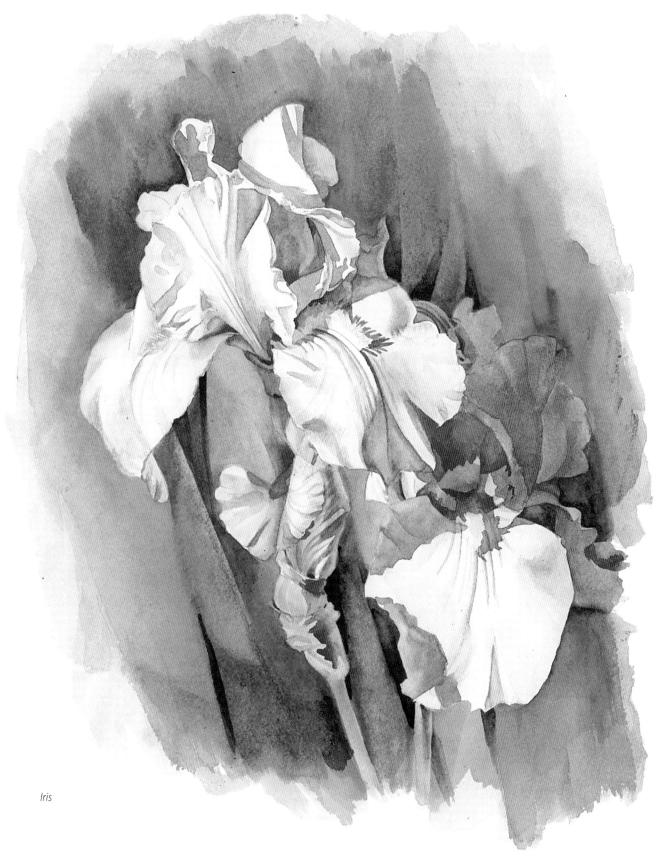

Iris

Stems and Leaves

While we usually think of all stems as slender cylinders, there can be subtle differences even between related forms. There are as many different stems and leaves as there are flowers.

Often beautiful leaf arrangements are the focus of floral paintings. Close-up views of palm fronds lend themselves to semi-abstract designs. Fig leaves are exceptionally handsome. Some leaves look like long blades. Carnation leaves curl out from either side of the stem like upside-down cup hooks. Leaves can be pad-dle-shaped, circular disks. Observation is the key. Carelessly drawn or painted leaves can ruin an otherwise lovely floral painting.

Sometimes stems may not be visible in a crowded bouquet, but the flowers must always appear to be supported by logically placed stems. Obviously, you don't want to paint every stem, but you do want to suggest their presence. Stems or leaves that are carelessly placed can leave a viewer with an uncomfortable feeling.

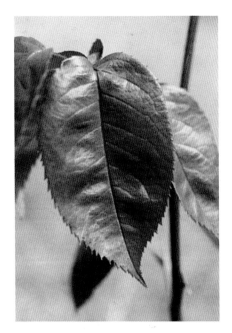

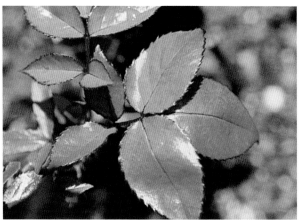

New leaves of some roses are reddish in hue, while others begin as varicolored or green. Most of the roses I know of have leaves with saw-toothed edges. Notice that the edges of the green leaves are red, as is the central vein and stem.

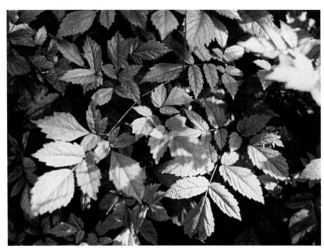

At first glance, these leaves may look like rose leaves. However, the saw-toothed edges are more pronounced, and the leaves, more slender. These are the leaves of an entirely different plant. See how a carelessly drawn leaf might diminish your painting?

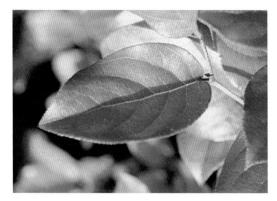

Salad leaves are thick and crisp. Florists sometimes use them as fillers. Their stems zigzag between each leaf and in the spring the stems, as well as the leaf's edges, have a rosy hue. Leaves are beautiful—they deserve as much attention as the flowers.

Include Everything

Take time to study the flowers you intend to paint. When you think you have finished your drawing, go back and look again at your subject. There may be more to see. In my workshops, when I point out a line or a shape that has been overlooked, the response is usually "Oh yes, I can see that!"

Learning to see is the first obligation of an artist. The rewards are many. Seeing as an artist will not only open the door to better painting, but it will also increase your wonder and enjoyment of the beauty of nature.

Intellectually, we all are aware of the three-dimensional world in which we live, and we want to suggest that three-dimensional world in our florals. In this book you will see that every flower, stem and leaf has its beginning as a basic form.

At least some of the stems in the midst of the bouquet must appear to be extensions of those in front.

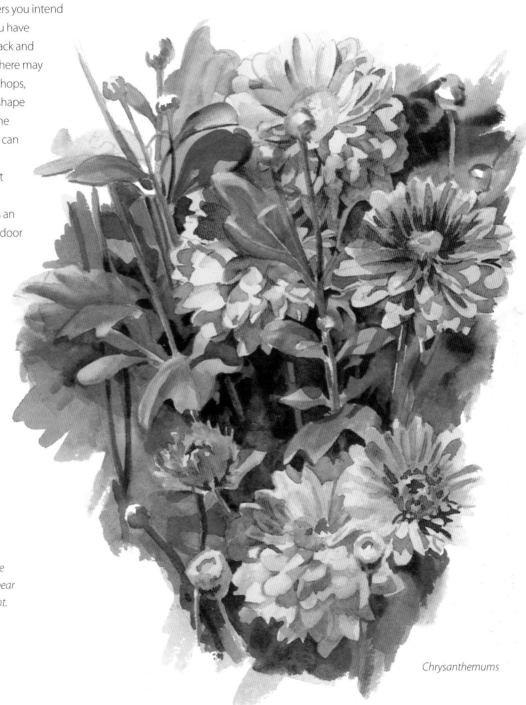

Chrysanthemums

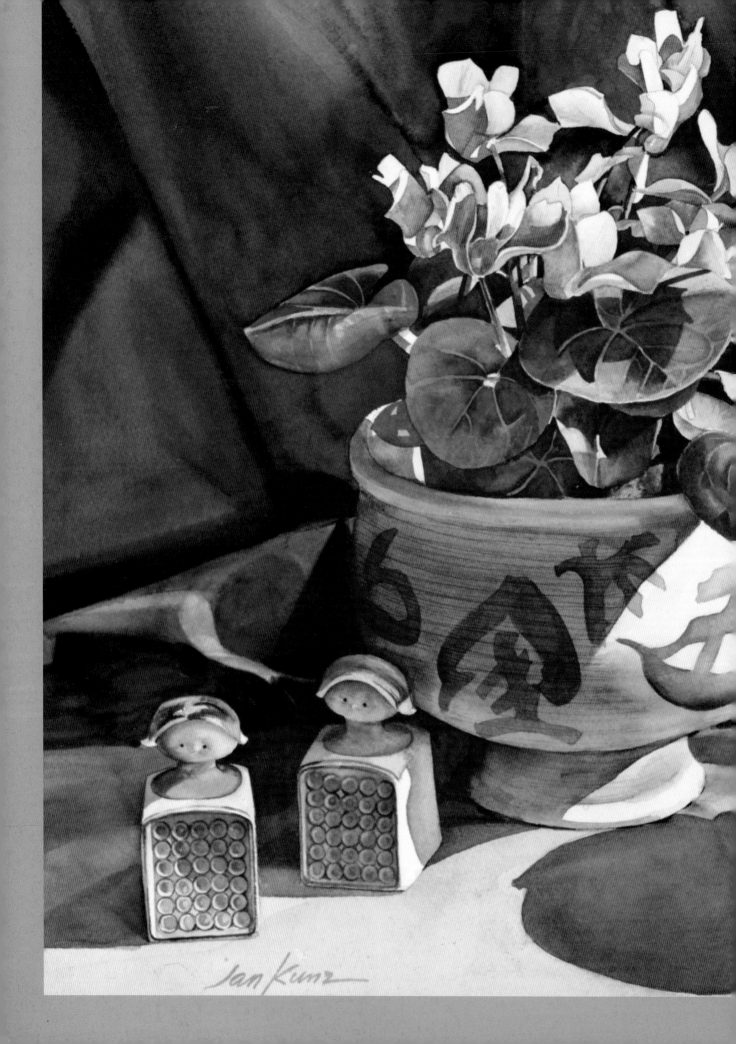

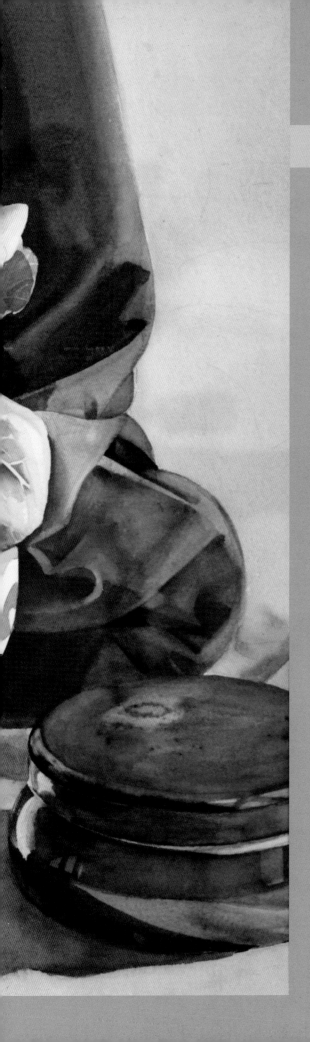

4

Painting Flowers From Life

Painting from life can be a totally delightful experience. Painting outdoors is even more fun, especially if a basket lunch is close at hand! Whether indoors or out, finding the right subject is the first concern.

I think the best subjects are those that jump up before your eyes and say "paint me!" Usually it is the light, color, or dark-and-light pattern that attracts us, rather than any particular subject.

Painting in a quiet garden on a sunny day can be pure enjoyment. However, if "getting a picture" is your goal, your concentration may be better in your studio (or on the kitchen table). Painting in the field is great fun, but the wind, changing light and accompanying insects provide numerous distractions.

Cyclamen and Shakers
20" × 20" (51cm × 51cm)

Where to Look for Flowers

It has been my experience that people enjoy sharing their gardens. If you ask for permission to paint their flowers, they may invite you to stay, and perhaps offer you a bouquet. Even your local nurseryman may permit you to paint in his display yard. Also, farmer's markets and flea markets are other places you'll likely find flowers to paint.

Almost every city has an area where artisans meet to share their crafts. Flowers, fresh or dried, are often part of the display.

Unusual Locations

No doubt you already know the best place to find flowers in your neighborhood, but here are a couple of suggestions you may not have considered.

Funeral directors sometimes have leftover floral arrangements. A church may have altar pieces that won't last until the next service. Perhaps you know someone in a restaurant who could rescue any abandoned table decorations. A persistent artist is a force to be reckoned with!

Other Possibilities

I prefer to paint old-fashioned, familiar flowers. Rose, lilacs, pansies, carnations and countless others have been favorites for as long as I can remember.

Don't overlook the possibilities for design offered by many succulents. Also, jimsonweed, cat tails and skunk cabbage are all beautiful. You can create unique and colorful arrangements using such subjects as cabbage, artichokes, corn and corn husks, wheat, thistle, branches, pinecones, leaves and mushrooms. The list is almost endless.

There are some remarkably beautiful silk flowers on the market these days. Arrangements made of silk flowers have the added advantage of not wilting or fading under strong light.

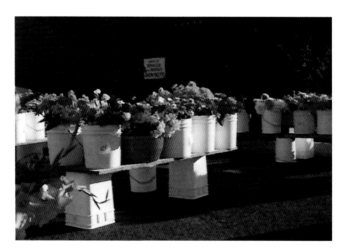

Flowers at a farmer's market in Albany, Oregon, are just waiting for a painter to discover them.

Familiar flowers, such as these rhododendrons, roses and daisies, are always popular subjects for floral paintings.

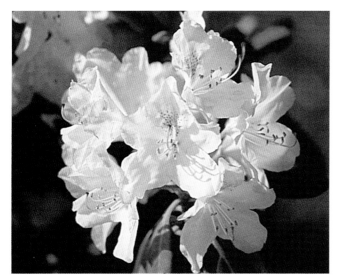

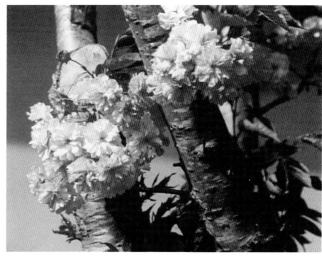

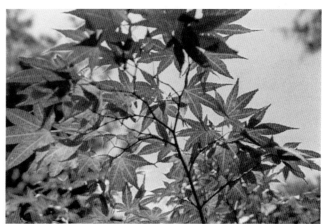

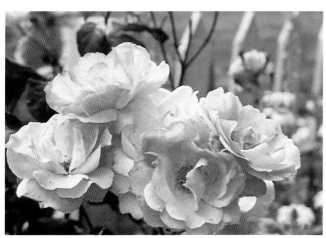

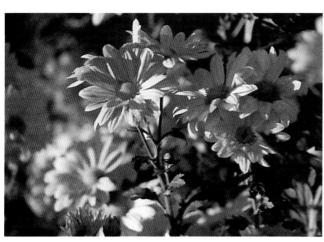

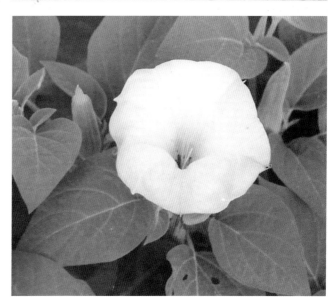

Cherry blossoms, autumn leaves, wildflowers and weeds are other possible subjects for a floral painting.

Floral Arranging

Don't begin painting until you are satisfied with the overall shape and distribution of color within your floral arrangement, as well as the placement of the props.

Props

If you are looking for props, it's possible to find interesting vases, glass canning jars, bottles or other objects you might use in floral setups at garage sales or in used furniture stores.

Any props you use should enhance your subject and never overwhelm it! Be sure that each object you include echoes a theme, and always avoid the temptation to include unrelated objects, no matter how beautiful they may be.

Presentation

Take advantage of people's tendency to associate flowers with special occasions. Flowers along with open boxes and a profusion of ribbons suggest a party. A corsage and a dance card might recall a wonderful evening. Wildflowers in a canning jar could be reminiscent of a friendly farm kitchen.

The way you present your flowers is important. Try to feel empathy for your setting.

Think about textures. Rough pottery containers, porcelain vases and baskets, along with a variety of other containers, offer opportunities for textural contrast.

Arranging

Arranging flowers is something like planting a garden. You don't plant flowers just anywhere. For instance, keep the daisies together and perhaps add larkspur in another clump with a sprinkling of still another variety to connect them.

Try to place the flowers in various positions so that there are blooms visible from several angles. Some flowers have a way of staring straight at you, so try to tilt them in such a way as to divert their view.

Study your arrangement, and if things look cluttered, try substituting stems or blossoms for pots. In short, make sure the arrangement feels comfortable.

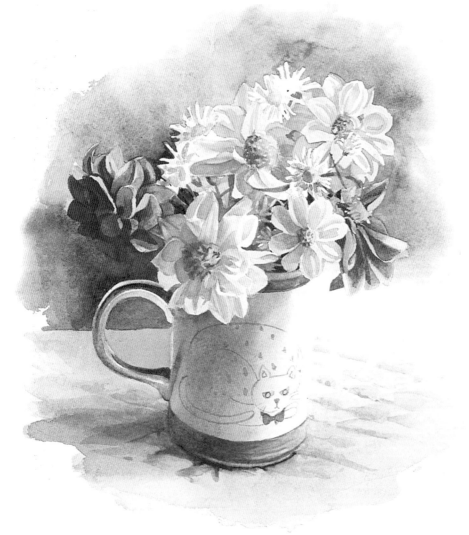

Flowers in a cup on my drawing board became a subject for a painting.

Viewpoint

Before you settle for a straight-on view, look at your floral arrangement from different eye levels. Try placing your arrangement slightly above (or below) your line of sight. Point of view can make a difference.

Close-up views of flowers or plants are a never-ending source of beautiful design. In the hands of an artist like Georgia O'Keeffe, one flower can inspire a masterpiece.

Lighting

Lighting is a major consideration in any setup. Remember, light must come from one direction and only one direction. I said that twice for emphasis! Whatever light illuminates your setup should also illuminate your painting area. If you let light come from more than one source, the light and shadow areas will become confusing.

I think it is best to arrange the light so it comes from one side of the setup. In this way each object in your arrangement has a dark and a light side. Straight-on lighting tends to make objects appear flat.

Look at these photos of dried leaves. I'm sure you will agree that the "straight-on" lighting and viewpoint is far less dramatic than the backlit arrangement with a "seen from above" viewpoint.

Always set up your arrangement under the same light you intend to use. In the final analysis, *it is the pattern of light and dark shapes you are arranging!*

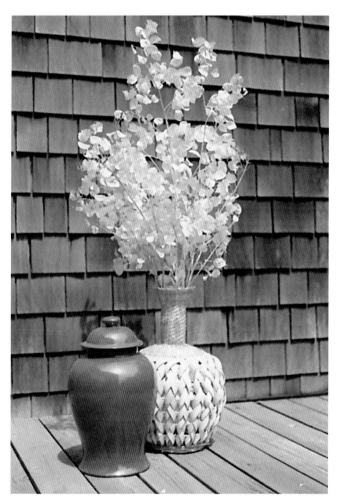

Straight-on lighting tends to make objects appear flat.

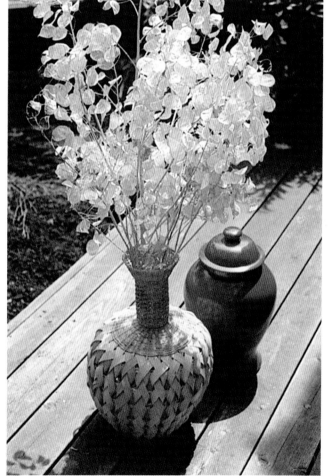

Imaginative lighting combined with an unusual viewpoint can add drama to any arrangement.

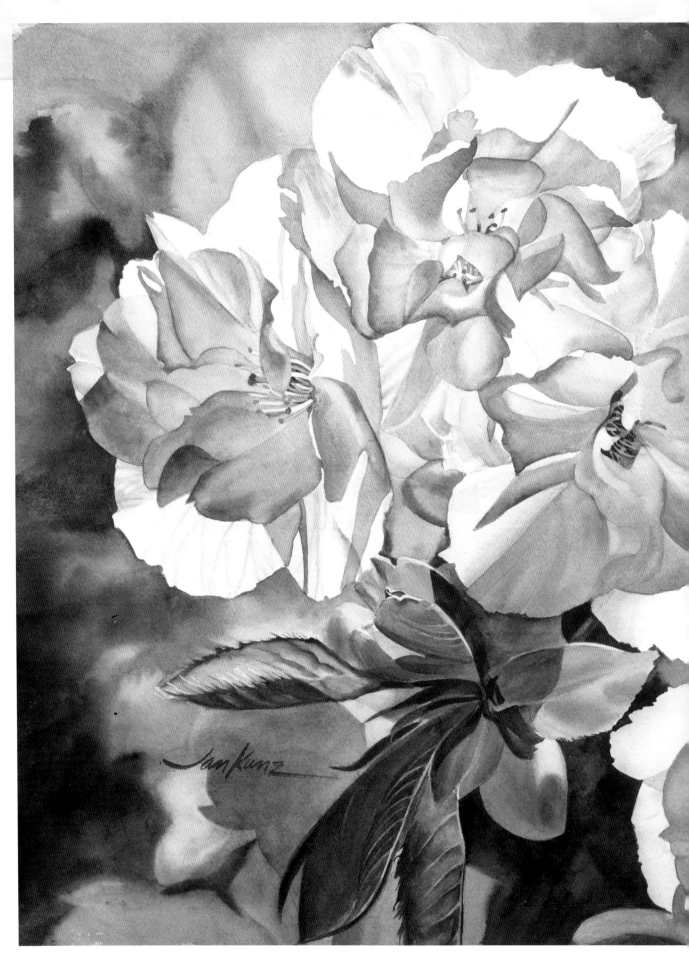

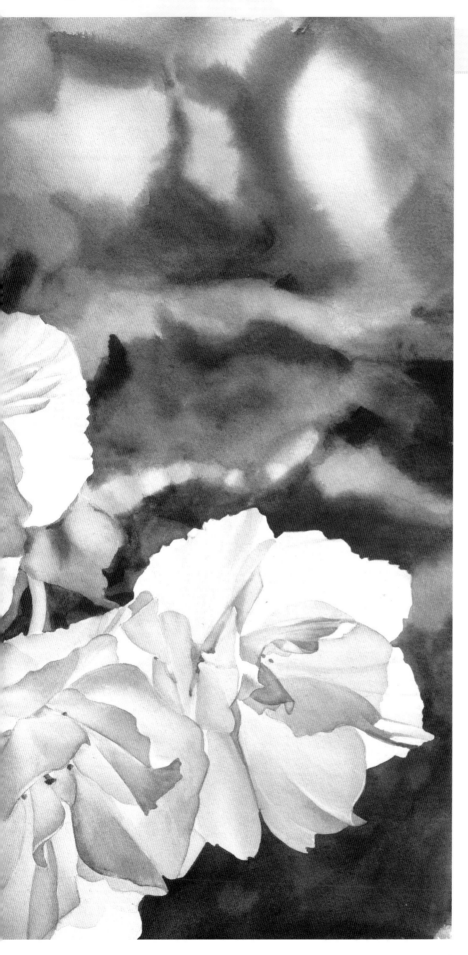

Backlighting, rather than standard toplighting, is one way to add interest and drama to your florals. Many flowers and leaves can appear translucent under the right lighting conditions. Backlighting works well with flowers that have especially translucent petals.

Mt. Fuji Cherry Blossoms
22" × 30" (56cm × 76cm)

Building a Stage

It is easy to use an ordinary cardboard carton to construct a simple stage for your floral arrangement or still-life setup.

Cut the carton so as to leave the bottom and two adjacent sides. The sides become the background, and the bottom is the stage for your floral arrangement. If your box is a bit small, it is an easy matter to extend the sides or bottom with matboard or craft paper. Next, select the props to include and decorate the stage to your liking. You are the stage manager!

Place the box so the light strikes one side of the background and the other is in shadow. With this setup, you can arrange the objects so their shadow side is seen against the sunny plane of the background and the sunny side of the objects stands out against the adjoining dark background.

This basic principle of light against dark and dark against light makes each form easily recognizable. You can achieve other lighting effects by simply putting a cover across your stage setup.

Once everything is in place, photograph your arrangement. Time goes so quickly when you paint that the flowers may begin to fade before you know it. With your photograph for reference, you have the security of knowing your arrangement will last as long as you need it.

Materials

SUPPLIES
Cardboard
Sharp knife
Blue mat board
Objects, flowers, etc.

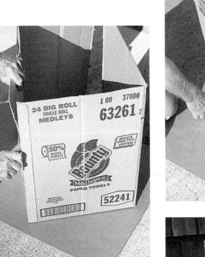

1 Cut the Carton
Use a sharp knife to cut down along opposite corners of a large cardboard carton.

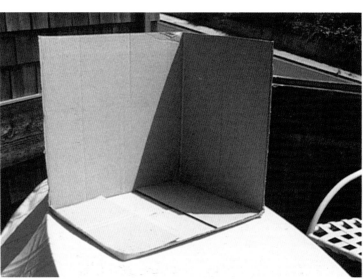

2 Remove the Sides
Cut along the bottom edge to remove two adjacent sides of the box. The remaining two sides and bottom of the cardboard carton become a stage for your floral arrangement.

3 Face the Light
Place the stage so one surface faces the light and the other is in shadow. It is now ready to be decorated with your floral arrangement.

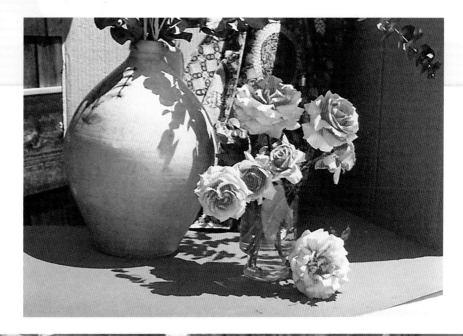

4 Decorate the Set

I added blue mat board for more color and draped a piece of fabric across the back. Next came a jug of dried leaves. The blue leaves repeated the color of the floor, and their shadow made an interesting pattern across the jug's surface. Finally, I added a vase of roses in the foreground.

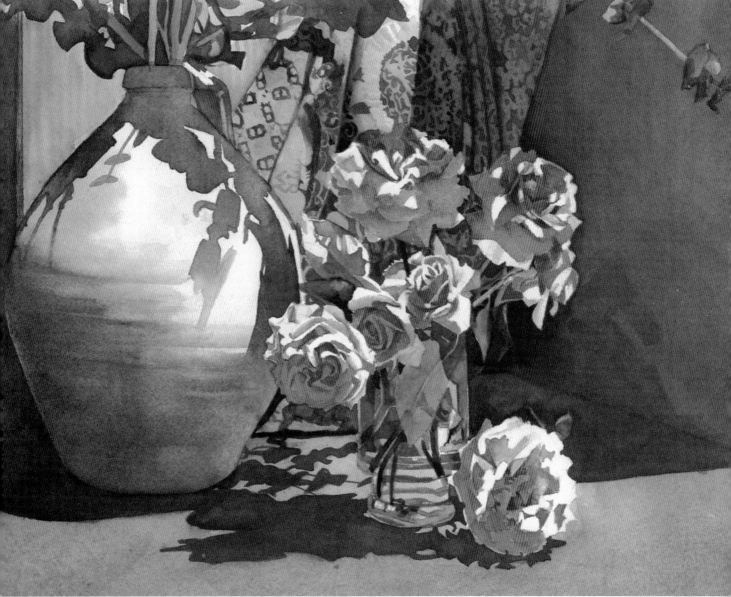

Here is my painting from this stage setup.

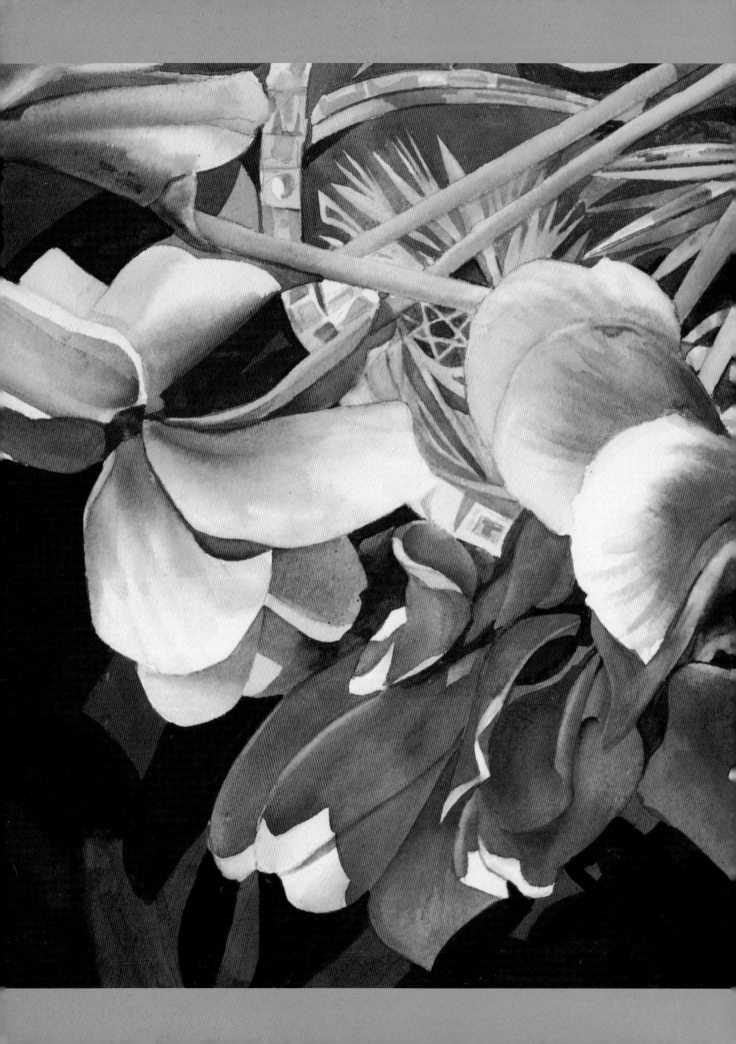

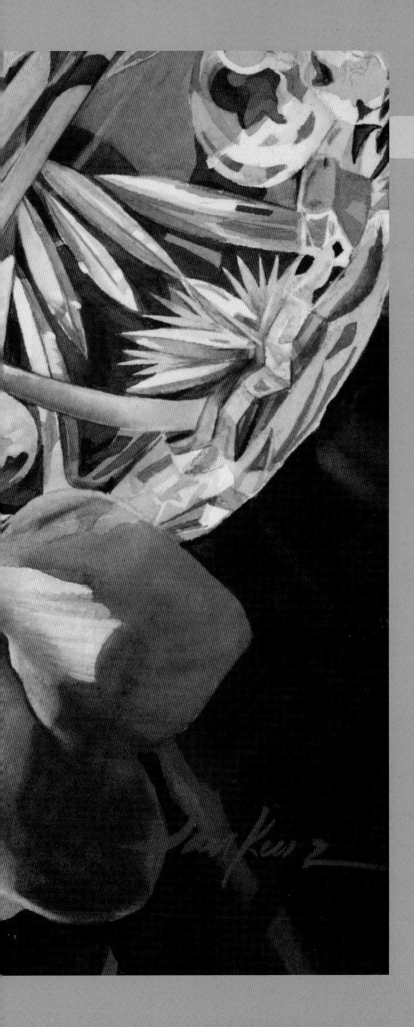

CHAPTER FIVE

Painting Flowers From Photographs

All summer long I keep my sketch pad and camera at the ready. The flowers I record during the summer months provide painting material for the dark winter days. Most artists, at one time or another, use photographs as reference material. Gathering photos of flowers ensures a constant supply of painting material. Not only do they make it possible to paint when fresh flowers are not available, but they can provide an opportunity to combine images from one or several photos into a new composition.

The flowers in photographs don't wilt and they stay in position so you can study their form as well as the nuances of light and color. Photos of flowers, along with other scrap material, can provide almost unlimited painting material. "Cyclamen in Crystal" was painted from a section of a photo.

Cyclamen in Crystal
22" × 30" (56cm × 76 cm)

Acquiring a Scrap Collection

Today, most artists have an extensive scrap file. If you haven't already organized a scrap file, doing so may save you hours of searching for a particular item.

What is a Scrap File?

A scrap file is a collection of photographs, newspaper clippings, magazine ads, sketches, or whatever a painter might use as reference material. My file includes everything from a wagon wheel to a table

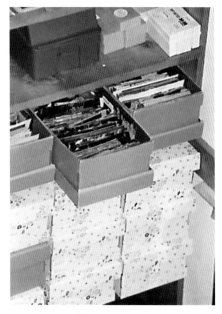

This is how I used to store my photographs! Each open shoe box is full of photos and the closed shoe boxes on the shelf below contain slides. Each box is labeled on the outside.

setting. I often get painting ideas from merely scanning through the photographs and other material that I have collected.

Digital Photography

Digital photography has made the gathering of photographic scrap material easier than ever before. The use of film and slides has become almost obsolete.

We no longer have to wait until our film is developed to see if we were able to get the pictures we wanted. Digital cameras let us know instantly if we need to try again for the perfect shot.

Using Photographs

Photographs offer another advantage outside of the scrap pile. If you study a photograph carefully, you may begin to notice nuances of color and form not apparent through casual observation. Perhaps you can spot reflected light you hadn't seen before, or a place where light from behind has caused a petal to become translucent. When you work from photos, you can work at your leisure and take time to experiment.

Photographs help you gather subject material. But the way you organize and present this material should be uniquely your own. When you paint from life, you design your work and paint the things that make for good design. The same must hold true when you work from photos. Don't

ever feel compelled to include everything in the photo. Pick and choose the elements that will help you create a pleasing composition, and rearrange them in the most pleasing way.

Storing Your Scrap File

Many artists take advantage of the immense capacity of their computers to house their scrap file. Now it is a simple matter to store photos and scanned clippings into a computer in such a fashion that they are easily retrievable.

For instance, I download my photos and scanned material to my computer and put them into appropriate categories. I have a separate file for daisies, roses and another for tree blossoms. I can even "flag" a photo of special interest for instant recall. In addition to all the other advantages, I can even make prints of this resource material without leaving the studio.

There are hundreds of ways to store information How you store it isn't important. What is important is that it works for you. As impossible as it seems, I used to store my scrap material in shoe boxes. Over the years we will no doubt find new ways to store and manage our files, but you will always find that a good scrap file can be a real asset.

Photographing Flowers

My experience with photography is limited. I am no photo expert, but I am able to get good photos with my Nikon Coolpix P90 camera. This camera can do a great deal more than I ask of it, like taking movies or shooting sports events at high speed. To me the best part is the large viewing area that permits me to arrange my composition before I snap the picture, along with the instant recall feature that lets me see what I have recorded. The zoom lens magnifies up to twenty-five times so even the blossoms on the top of the tree are brought sharply into view.

It's best to take flower photos on a sunny day. It has been my experience that even a light overcast can dull the brilliance and clarity of the color. The morning and afternoon hours provide the best shadow angles.

Remember to take photos of the stems, leaves, thorns, etc. Be sure to record how the flower is attached to the stem and how the leaves grow. You may need this kind of information.

Pitfalls to Avoid

Flat Lighting The photos of flowers you find, for example, in seed catalogs generally make poor subject matter. These photos are usually taken "straight on" with midday lighting, and there is little or no shadow. We need shadow shapes to help create the illusion of a solid form and to create beautiful patterns in our floral paintings.

Panoramic Views Fields of flowers are beautiful to see, but I do not recommend them as the basis for a floral painting. Such photos may be useful as material for

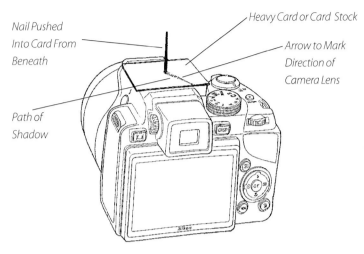

THE "NEVER-FAIL NAIL"
The shadow of a nail pushed through a piece of heavy paper or business card) will mark the direction of the light. The arrow points in the same direction in the camera's lens.

backgrounds in landscape paintings, or as the basis for abstract patterns. It is much easier to create a floral painting with a few blooms and a closer view.

Scattered Look Often, the flowers you find to photograph in a garden have a way of being separated from one another. Flowers seldom arrange themselves into paintable groups. Unless you plan to paint a single flower, you must be careful to avoid a scattered look. Your floral painting must never look as if it were designed by a shotgun blast or as the pattern for wallpaper.

The "Never-fail Nail"

It's very likely that at times you'll find it necessary to photograph several flowers (or one from several different angles) to get enough material. If these photos are for use in the same painting, the light in each photo must come from the same direction. This can be surprisingly confusing. On these occasions I use my "never-fail nail." Just push a nail through a business-size card so that it pokes up vertically through the center. Draw an arrow on the card and point the arrow in the direction you intend to take the picture. Next, check the direction of the shadow cast by the nail. Be sure the shadow is in the same place on the card every time you take a picture. In this way you can be sure, no matter how many photos you take, the light will always be from the same direction.

Combining Photographs

Combining the images in different photographs is an excellent way to use your photo collection to find exciting new floral subjects.

After you've chosen parts of several photographs that you'd like to use, the next step is to combine them to make an interesting composition. A shortcut to exploring several floral arrangement possibilities is to place a piece of frosted acetate or tracing paper over the photo(s) and trace the flowers you want to use.

When you have drawn several flowers on separate pieces of acetate, you are ready to rearrange them into a new composition by simply superimposing them upon one another and moving them around until you like what you see.

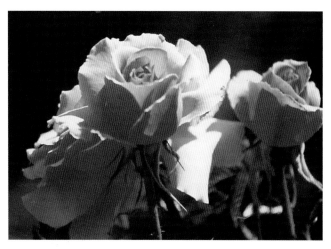

Photo no. 1

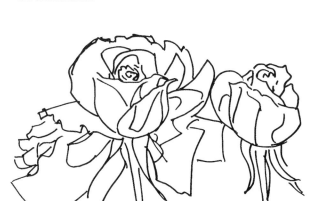

The elements of photo no.1 were traced onto one piece of frosted acetate.

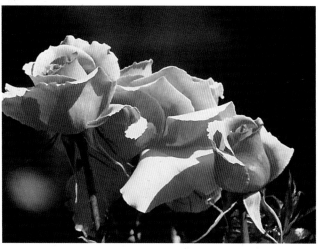

Photo no. 2

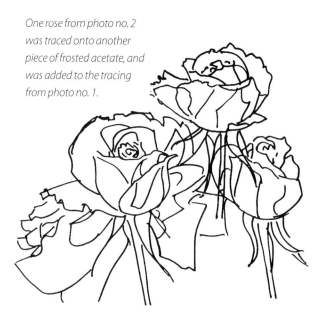

One rose from photo no. 2 was traced onto another piece of frosted acetate, and was added to the tracing from photo no. 1.

The combined drawings were rearranged to form a new composition. Notice I've adjusted the roses slightly into a tighter grouping.

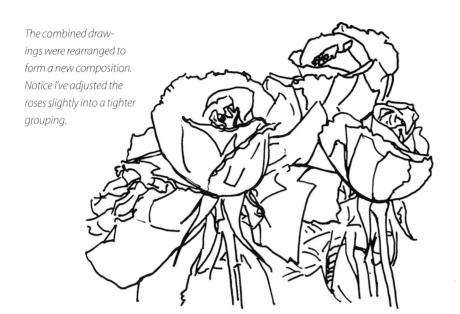

Finally, here's my watercolor sketch made from the new composition of a combination of elements in photos 1 and 2. The photos helped me keep the direction of the sunlight and shadows consistent. Because the direction of light is the same in both, I was free to use any part of either photo to compose the painting.

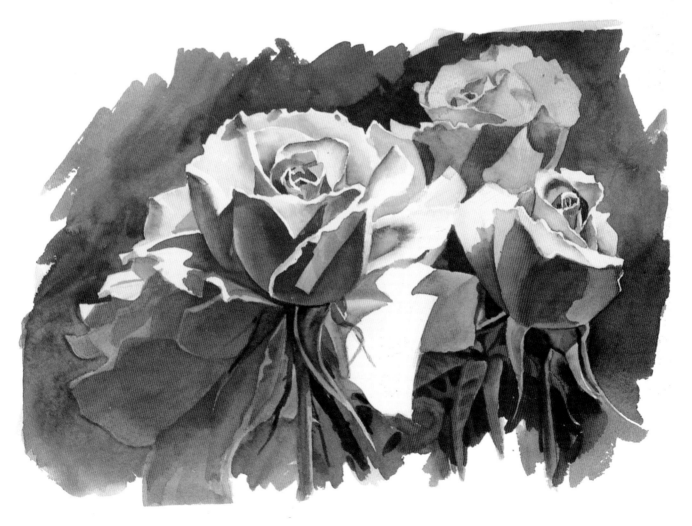

Several Paintings from One Photo

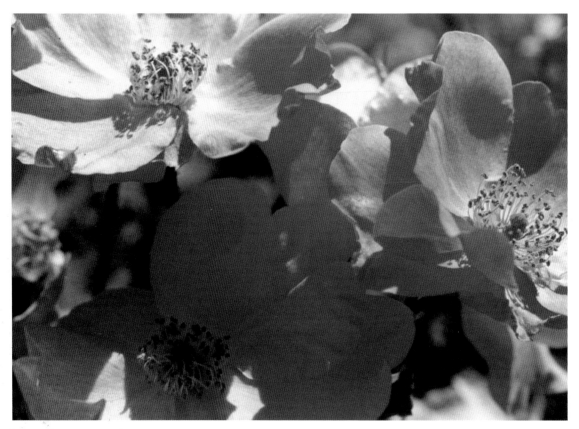

It is possible to find material for several paintings within one photograph.

Often you can find two or three beautiful floral designs within just one photograph. Make a couple of small mat corners from a piece of stiff paper and do some exploring in your photographs. In this photo, I found three designs almost immediately. This is a lot of fun, and you may be inspired to paint your first abstract!

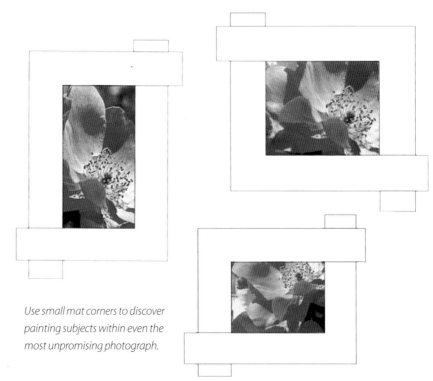

Use small mat corners to discover painting subjects within even the most unpromising photograph.

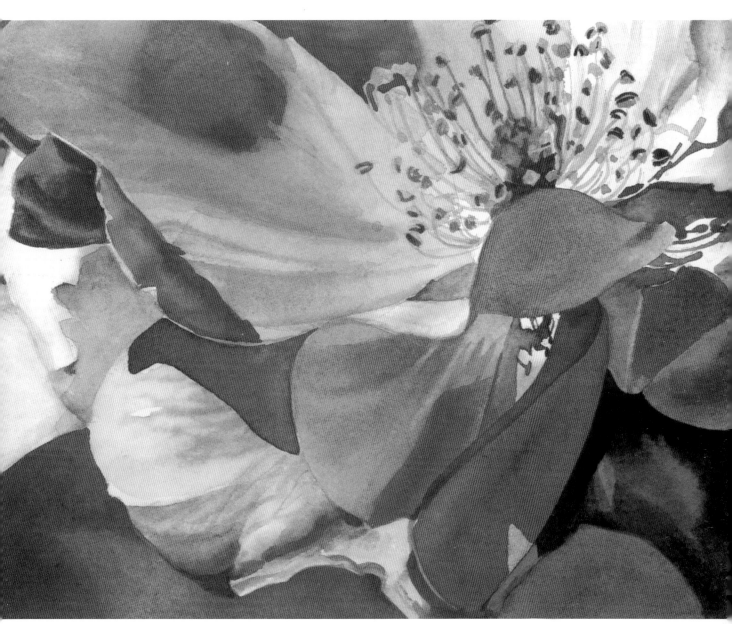

This is the abstract painting I did from a cropped portion of the photograph.

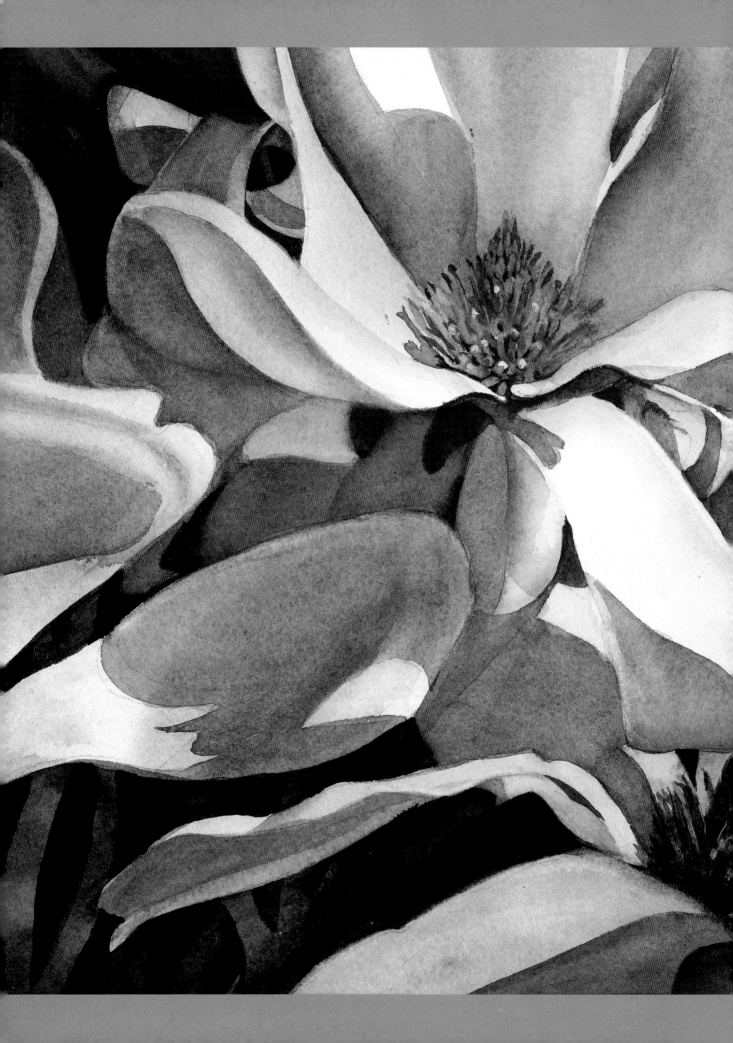

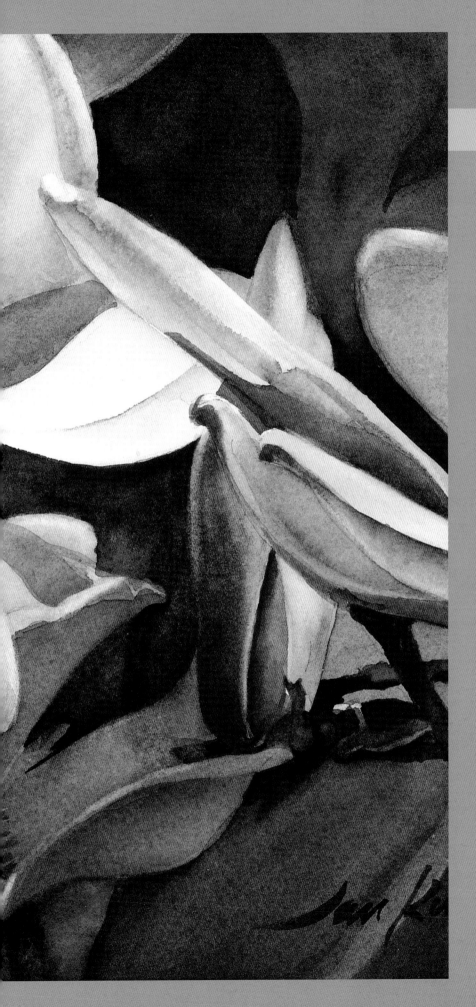

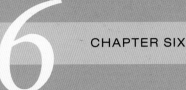

CHAPTER SIX

Composing a Dynamic Floral Painting

In simple terms, composition means selecting the elements you want in your painting and arranging them effectively. A well-planned composition is essential to a beautiful painting. No amount of fancy brushwork can compensate for poor composition.

Many good books have been written on the subject of composition. Since the purpose of this book is to teach floral painting, I will leave the in-depth discussion of the elements and principles of composition to others. We will concentrate here on how these elements apply to painting flowers.

Moonlight Magnolias
10" × 18" (25cm × 46cm)

Composition

Composition is one of those subjects that, once understood, seems simple, but trying to explain it is like participating in the Abbott and Costello comedy routine "Who's on first"!

The Elements

The tools we use in art are line, value, color, texture, direction, size and shape. These tools are called the elements of composition. To achieve a unity of design, we must use these tools to tell only one story. In other words, some element must dominate the composition.

For example, suppose we were to paint an overall pattern of daisies. The repeated shape of the daisy would dominate the composition, and we would achieve design unity. We would have created a harmonious design because all of the shapes would be similar. However, our painting might be dull and uninteresting.

Adding Contrast

Like Tabasco sauce in cooking, the zing is added when an element of contrast is introduced. For example, we might add excitement to our painting of daisies by adding contrasting straight lines—let's say a picket fence. Design unity would be maintained so long as the picket fence was kept subordinate to the daisies.

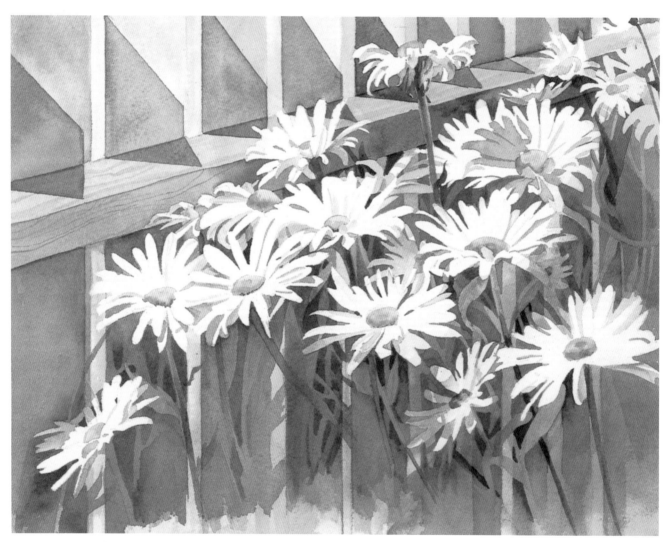

The repeated shape of the daisies is made more exciting by the contrasting straight lines of the fence.

Backyard Daisies
10" × 12½" (25cm × 32cm)

Designing Your Picture Area

The area between the boundaries of your watercolor paper is the picture area. You have already dealt with picture area if you have ever taken a photograph. When you look through the viewfinder of your camera, you have to decide what to place within that little rectangle. Perhaps you want to include all of your subject. Perhaps you want to step in for a close-up view. In the same way, you have to decide how large to make the important elements of your painting, and where to place them in order to make the most effective use of the picture area.

There are a few simple things to remember when you compose your picture. The objects must fit well into the picture area, not be unduly crowded toward any edge. In most instances, objects should appear comfortably placed. For example, you would not draw a vase too near the edge of a table.

Common Sense Composition

The sketches illustrate how a composition can be improved by applying simple common sense.

The first attempt at composing the still life is very weak. The gift bag, glass of roses and ribbon are all located in the center of the composition. The glass and roses conceal the gift bag and leave it almost uniden-

tifiable. The negative space on either side of these central objects is nearly the same size and totally uninteresting. A ribbon, which could be used to draw the eye into the composition, lies tangent with the bottom of the bag and becomes a meaningless addition.

Moving the glass of roses and the gift bag farther apart makes these objects easy to identify. This move, plus the addition of a leaf, improves the shape of the background space. The ribbon still does not relate to the rest of the

composition and tends to lead the eye in and out of the composition.

In the final sketch, I used the ribbon to lead the eye into the picture and to connect the various shapes. Better background (negative) shapes were created by moving the bag farther to the left.

Make it easy for your viewer to understand and enjoy what you have to show him. Be sure every object is easy to identify.

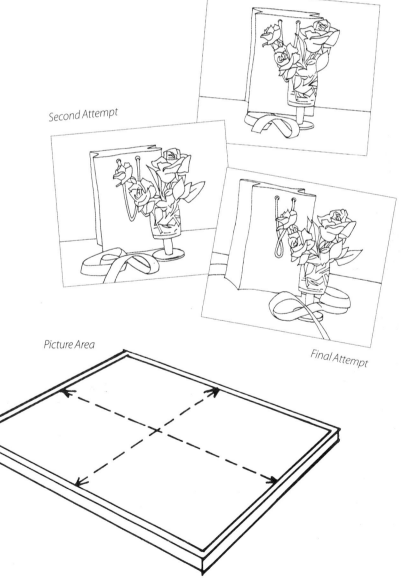

First Attempt

Second Attempt

Final Attempt

Picture Area

Creating Dominance

If you put only one object, no matter how small, in your composition, that object will be the center of interest, and the eye will be drawn to it. Things don't get tricky until you include other objects. Then you have to decide on their relative importance. Something must dominate so the viewer will know what you are trying to show him or her. You will use the principle of dominance along with other design principles to create your paintings.

Dominance by Repeated Shapes

In the sketch below, dominance is achieved by the repeated use of curved shapes. Not only do the pots and vase have curved sides, but this curved shape is repeated throughout the composition. The element of contrast is introduced with the radiating forms of the branches.

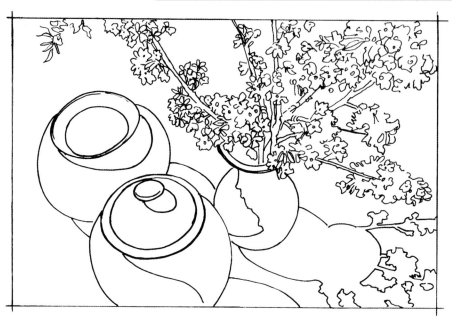

Repeated curved lines and shapes dominate this composition. The contrasting shapes of the branches and blossoms help provide interest.

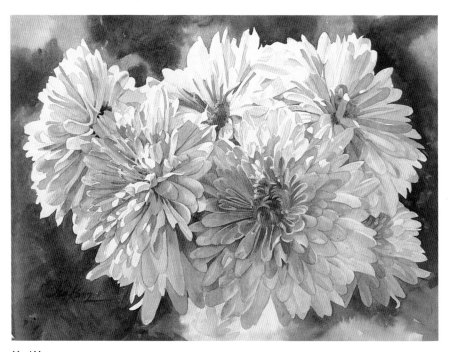

Maxi Mums
22" × 30" (56cm × 76cm)

Here the blossoms combine to create one dominant shape. The radiating petals provide interest.

Size and Dominance

You can vary the size of the objects in your composition to show what is important. One object can be made to overwhelm another, or dominate it only slightly, depending on their relative size. If you want your viewer's interest to be equally divided, you can make all objects the same size; but be aware, such a composition can easily become monotonous.

The branches in the sketch at the right dominate the composition. They overwhelm the secondary objects with their size and strong directional (radiating) lines.

When you use props or other objects in your composition, try to vary their size. Objects that are alike in size can appear uninteresting, even though they have different shapes.

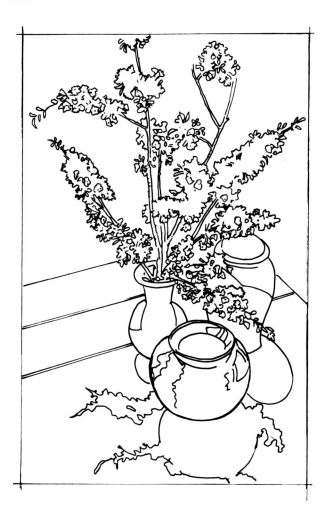

Blossoms radiating from the central vase are the dominant form because of their size and strong direction.

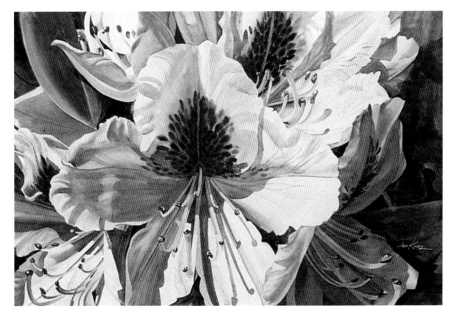

Rhodies
26" × 41" (66cm × 104cm)

This blossom dominates the picture plane because of its sheer size.

Creating Dominance

Overlapping and Dominance

Another way to achieve dominance is by overlapping shapes. One object can be made to appear more important by partly concealing a secondary object behind it.

Size

In this sketch, I have used both size and overlapping in an attempt to draw the eye to the largest pot in the foreground. But notice, something is wrong. The composition leaves you feeling slightly uneasy. The reason is that the contrasting elements demand too much attention.

Cover the top half of the sketch with your hand and the pot in the foreground becomes the dominant form I intended it to be. Design unity is restored.

Now look again at the sketch on the previous page. See what happens if you crop the top half of this sketch. Reduce the size of the branches and dominance is lost. Design chaos is the result.

We can make good use of the principle of overlapping shapes in planning our floral compositions. Many blossoms can be combined into a unified shape to dominate what might otherwise be a fragmented composition.

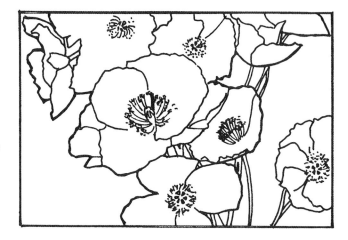

The overlapping shapes of many small flowers combine to create an interesting design. The linear stems add contrast and interest.

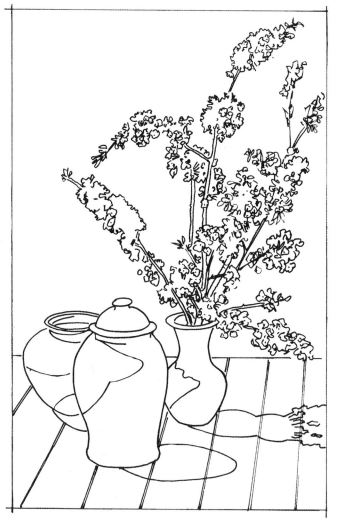

Competing shapes of near equal size diminish this composition.

Cropping

Large parts of secondary objects may be cropped by the boundariesof the picture area so long as the part remaining clearly identifies the object.

Depth

Drawing through objects as if they were transparent gives them room in space. Another way to suggest depth in your paintings is to make background objects smaller, or as we just saw, to overlap shapes in front of one another.

Try to place the objects in your composition so they make a varied, informal pattern in depth. Don't stop with your first idea; sometimes you can increase interest by trying something new. It often pays to experiment.

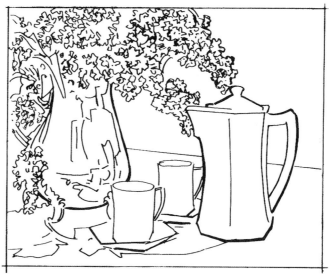

Cropping is still another way to overlap forms.

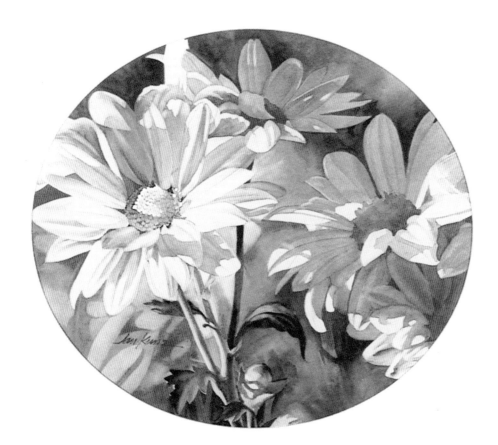

Sunny Daisies
18½" × 21" (47cm × 53cm)

The design principles of overlapping and cropping were both used in creating this painting of daisies.

By overlapping, the daisies' shapes were combined into one cohesive shape. Next, I used the borders of the painting to crop nonessential blooms, leaving only enough to suggest an abundance of flowers.

Creating Dominance

Value and Dominance

Value can be used in many ways to help your composition. For instance, value can draw the eye to the center of interest. Dark objects will stand out in a light area, or a light object can be placed next to a dark one for emphasis. Value works along with line, area (or size) and shape to build the composition.

You have probably heard the word *key* associated with a particular painting. Key refers to the overall value of a painting. A painting in which all of the values are at the light end of the scale is considered *high key*. The overall value of a painting can be a major factor in creating a mood. For instance, to create a mood of mystery, you might want all of the values to be dark, or *low key*. As you can guess, high-key paintings might evoke a happier mood. A full range of values means all the values from white to black are used. I believe watercolor is at its brilliant best when used in a full range of values.

It is very important to remember that value relationships should be consistent throughout your painting. Deciding on a simple value plan before you begin to paint can increase your chances for success.

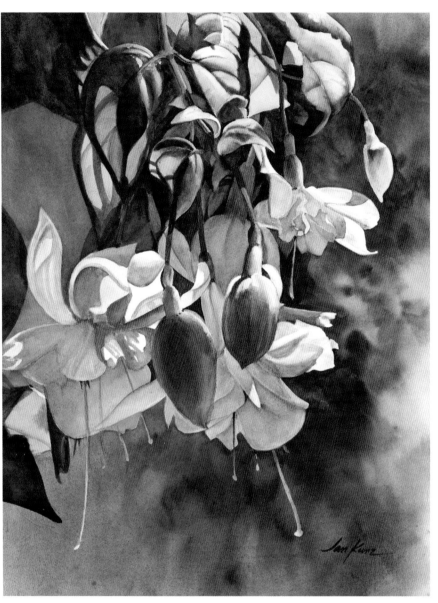

Fab Fuschia
22" × 18" (56cm × 46cm)

Pink dominates this composition even though there are many other strong competing hues.

We create directional kinds of lines with the objects in our paintings. By using line carefully, we can lead our viewer's eye through the composition.

Line can move the eye subtly and smoothly from one related object to another, or it can be a strong force resulting in an abrupt collision of lines. A line created by the edge of a table can forcefully direct the eye to the center of interest. Curved leaves or branches can be used to move the eye from one blossom to another.

Tony Couch, in his book *Watercolor, You Can Do It*, warned us to beware of the oblique. Strong diagonal lines can lead the eye out of the picture if they are not carefully planned. An art teacher once said, "If the lines in your painting point to the one hanging next to it, don't be surprised if no one looks at yours."

Study the direction of the lines in your sketch. Ask yourself: Do the main lines keep the eye within the picture area, and are they spaced at interesting intervals? Asking questions like these will help you plan a better painting.

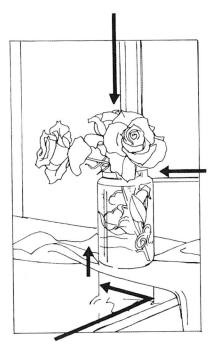

Use line to your advantage when you plan your composition.

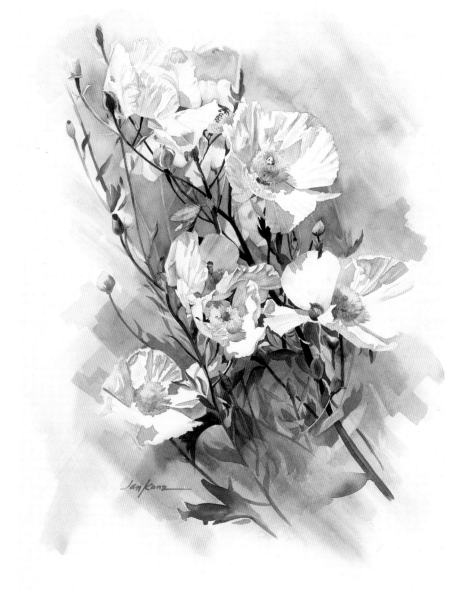

Spring Bouquet
30" × 22" (76cm × 56cm)

The strong directional thrust of the branch directs the eye from blossom to blossom across the page. Notice that the same value relationships are maintained on the branch as on the intersecting blossoms.

The S.A.T. Sketch

The purpose of an "S.A.T." (Stop and Think) sketch is to help you locate (and solve) potential problems before they confront you on your finished painting. For example, an S.A.T. sketch will force you to consider what you might do with the background before it jumps up to haunt you! My S.A.T. sketches are usually small (3" × 5" [8cm × 13cm]) pencil sketches.

Start Your Sketch

Begin with the basic forms of your subject matter. You don't want detail yet. The purpose of the sketch is to design the overall pattern of the picture area. Think about the possibility of using overlapping shapes or discovering a new point of view. This is the place to experiment.

After you are happy with the overall design, try placing a clean piece of tracing paper over your layout and making several value sketches until you are satisfied. I use vertical pencil lines to darken these shapes because it helps me to see pattern, not things. By using tracing paper overlays for your value sketches, you eliminate the need to redraw your initial plan with every sketch.

The S.A.T. Sketch and Your Photo

Let's suppose it's raining, and you have a great photograph of flowers you want to work from. You don't intend to do a preliminary sketch because you are going to do it just like the photo. Does that sound familiar? Chances are you may not have studied the photo carefully enough to spot problem areas, but no matter!

First, place a piece of tracing paper or frosted acetate (frosted acetate works better because it is more transparent) over your photo. Use a pencil to outline every shape you see. Ask yourself: Are there too many shapes? Are too many shapes the same size? Can I simplify or reduce the number of shapes by combining shapes of near equal value?

After you are satisfied, place a new piece of acetate over your simplified layout to work out your value plan. Make the darkest shapes very dark, and so on, until you have a value sketch of your photo. Here again, I suggest that you use vertical lines so you won't see objects—just dark and light shapes.

At first glance, the photograph of three pink roses might appear to be a great subject for a painting without any changes. But by taking ten or fifteen minutes to study the photo with the help of an acetate overlay, I found a few problem areas.

The rose on the left is separated from the other two blooms, leaving a dead space between them. Also, the strong diagonal wedge in the upper-right corner becomes more obvious.

A simple solution might be to enlarge the central rose, or add overlapping petals to eliminate the center void. The wedge could become another curved shape. Still another solution would be to move the two bottom roses more toward the center, and to gradate the background values from darker on the left to lighter on the right.

Why not try this method next time you are tempted to paint directly from a photo? I think you will be surprised at how many

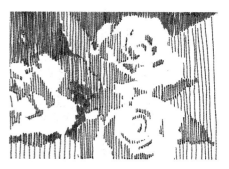

The simplified drawing identifies composition problems in this photo.

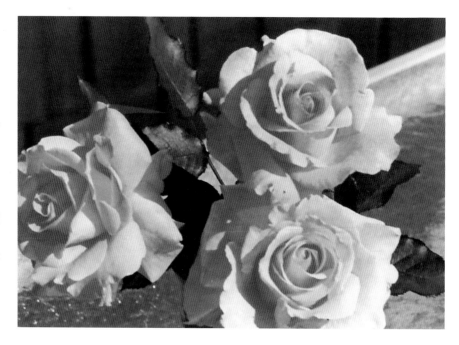

problems you will be able to recognize and solve before you begin to lay out your painting. A few minutes spent in planning can be the fastest way to a successful painting!

I don't remember the exact words, but Maitland Graves said in his book, *The Art of Color and Design*, that we may perceive and respond to the design of a picture more than we respond to subject matter! Good art requires good design.

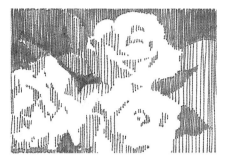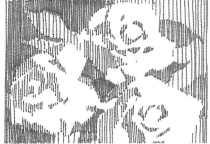

Here are two possible solutions to improve the design.

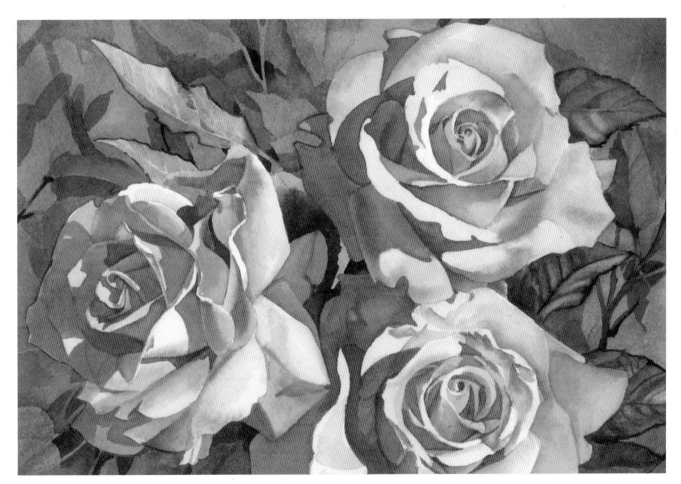

I decided the third S.A.T. sketch involved the problems in the photo, so I did my final painting from that. Compare the painting to the photo to see even subtle compositional changes can bring about remarkable results.

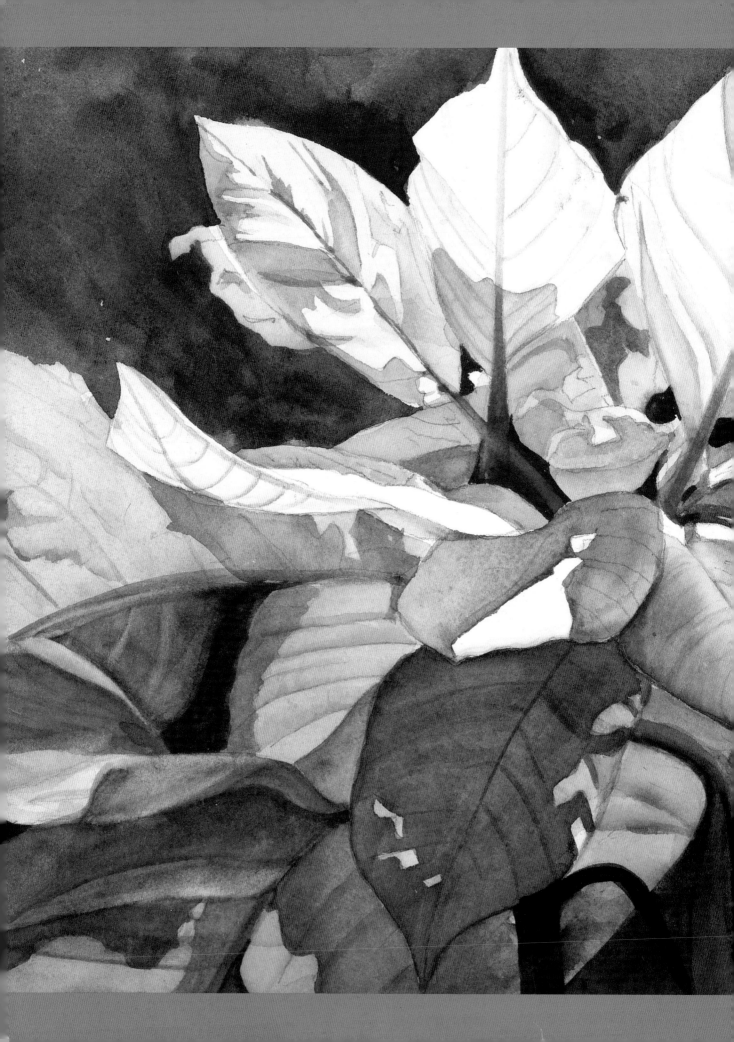

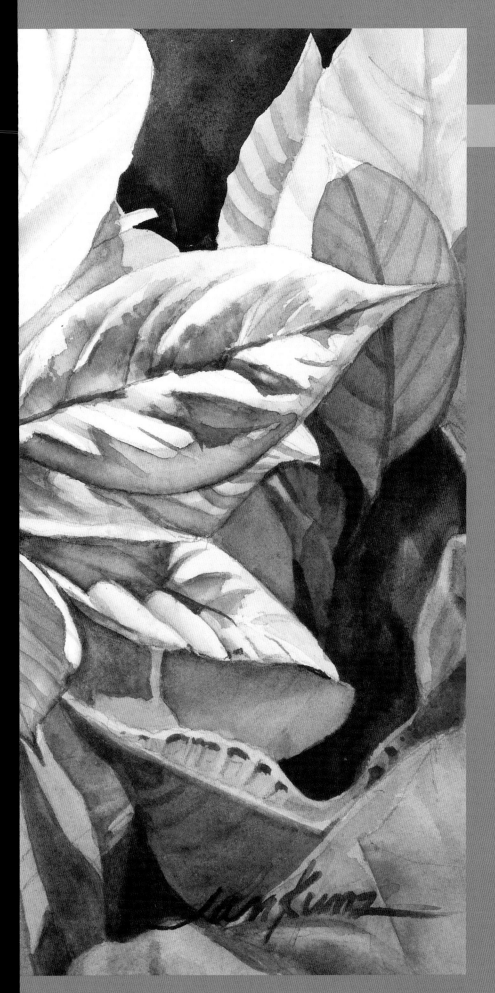

CHAPTER SEVEN

Painting the Illusion of Sunshine

Flowers and sunshine go together! We associate brilliance and color with floral paintings. So when you paint flowers, it is especially important to know how sunshine affects color. The photographs and paintings in this section will help you understand how to create the illusion of sunshine.

White Poinsettia
10" × 18" (25cm × 46cm)

Determining Value

Value refers to the lightness or darkness of a color. When you see a painter squinting at an object with eyes half-closed, he or she is probably trying to determine the object's value. When we squint, the hue becomes less dominant and we can see value.

If you have ever had a painting photographed in black and white, you know the importance of good value relationships. A picture without good value relationships will appear flat and uninteresting. Commercial artists are especially aware that value is by far the most important aspect of color. It is also the most important element in helping you portray sunlight.

Making a Value Scale

We can approximate value differences using an easy-to-make value scale. Scientists tell us the average human eye sees about ten or eleven distinct gradations in value. If we construct a chart with ten shades of gray evenly graded from white to black, using our off-white watercolor paper as value 1 and ending with black as value 10, we need only count up or down four values to arrive at a 40 percent difference. True, it won't be exact, but it will be near enough to ensure a successful representation of sunlight and shadow.

You can make your own value scale by painting scraps of watercolor paper with washes of any dark color (I use Payne's Gray). Gather ten evenly graded pieces ranging from white to black, and arrange and number them for easy comparison. You will have created a valuable tool.

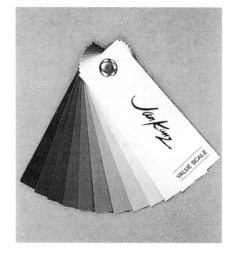

A value scale is a helpful tool in measuring value relationships. To paint the illusion of sunlight, first determine the value of your subject in sunlight. Count four values down to get the value the same object will appear in shadow. Then simply match the value of your color to the gray value. You will have a reasonably accurate illusion of sunlight.

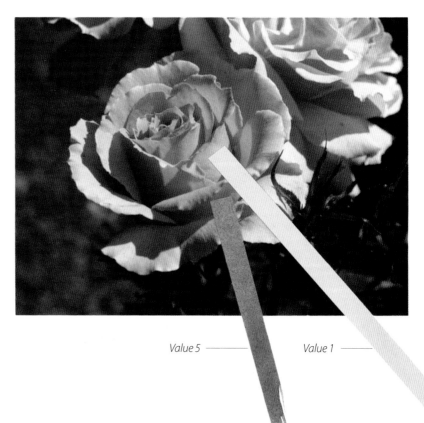

Value 5 —————   Value 1 —————

The 40 Percent Rule

Landscape painters observed long ago that, on sunny days, the shadow side of an object is a full 40 percent darker than the sunlit side. All things being equal (objects identical in hue, value and texture), the cast shadow is somewhat darker still. Even the shadow sides of clouds are 40 percent darker than their sunlit areas. After years of painting and careful observation, I have come to believe that this value relationship is a basic fact of nature.

Look at the roses on the facing page. The area in sunshine is value 1, and the part of the rose in shadow is 40 percent darker,

or value 5. The strips of watercolor I painted to match these values extend into the white area so you can see that this value difference is indeed accurate.

This same 40 percent value relationship holds true everywhere under the sun. When the local color is darker, the shadow will be darker, too. See how much darker the shadows on the green leaves and stems appear in the photos below of the fuchsia and poppies? This is because their local color is a darker value than the flowers they support.

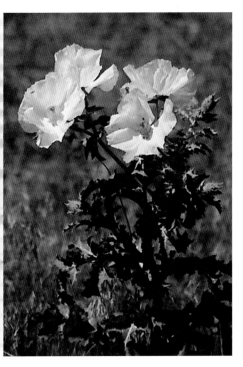

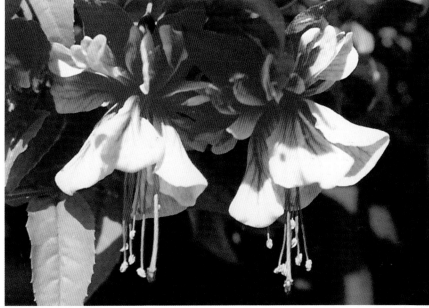

The value of the objects we see in sunshine will vary with their local color (the lightness or darkness of their actual pigment). The difference in value between the sunlit and shadow side is a constant. Above, the shadow side of the fuchsia is a mid-value because the local color pink is a very light value.

Sunlight and Color Temperature

The purpose of this section is to explain how the sharp light of the sun affects the color temperature of an object.

Color temperature is important to understand. We think of warm colors as those associated with fire. Yellow, orange and red are considered warm. Colors associated with water—blues and greens—are cool.

The following experiments are meant to duplicate various lighting conditions you may come across in nature. I used a white box to simplify the effects and because color temperature changes are most noticeable on a white surface. The photographs were taken outdoors in bright sunlight. The box is placed so that one side faces the sun and the cast shadow falls across a colored board beneath it.

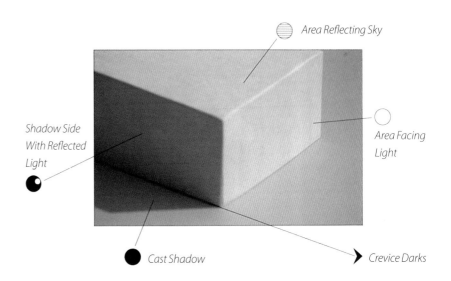

Area Reflecting Sky

Shadow Side With Reflected Light

Area Facing Light

Cast Shadow

Crevice Darks

SKY REFLECTIONS

The top of the box is cooler (more toward blue) than the vertical surface facing the light. This is because horizontal surfaces reflect the sky just as a pond reflects the sky on a sunny day. The value of the sunlit vertical side may be lighter or darker than the top of the box, but it will be warmer in hue (more toward orange). The side turned away from the light, like the top, is subject to the cool influence of the sky.

REFLECTED LIGHT

Reflected light can be any color and is not always obvious. In each box, we can see the lit surfaces, cast shadow and the shadow side of each box. We know the shadow side is 40 percent darker than the sunny side, but it is also subject to reflected light. The box on top is receiving a blue glow from the paper upon which it is placed. The box on the bottom is bathed in a rosy glow from a nearby piece of rose-colored paper. Observe the colors around your subject to give you a clue about possible reflected light on your subject.

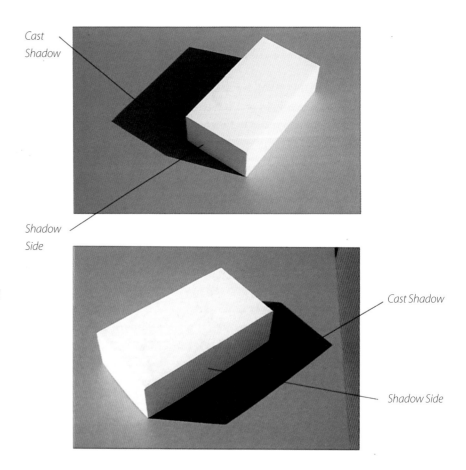

Cast Shadow

Shadow Side

Cast Shadow

Shadow Side

Shadows and Darks

On a bright sunny day you can learn a lot by observing the cast shadows of the objects around you. Look carefully and you will notice that the outermost edges of the shadow appear very dark and are cool in temperature. That is because your eyes are dazzled by the sharp value contrast between the sunlit and shadow side. If you walk into the shadow area you begin to see more color and notice more detail. It is possible to suggest this phenomenon by using dark, cool colors on the outer edges of shadow shapes and (without changing value) warmer hues in the center area.

Cast Shadows

The cast shadow is the same hue as the surface upon which it falls, and it is 40 percent-plus darker than the surrounding sunlit area. If the surface on which the cast shadow falls is dark, the shadow will be near black. Cast shadows do not contain reflected light.

Crevice Darks

Last, but very important, are the very small darks you see under the box at the edges. I call these crevice darks. These dark cracks are not affected by the sky; therefore, they are very warm. We will use the warm darks to great advantage when we paint the crevices and folds of petals.

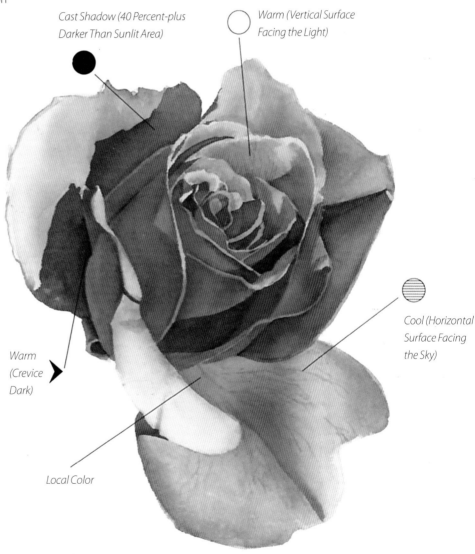

Cast Shadow (40 Percent-plus Darker Than Sunlit Area)

Warm (Vertical Surface Facing the Light)

Cool (Horizontal Surface Facing the Sky)

Warm (Crevice Dark)

Local Color

Although more complex in shape and form, a sunlit rose follows the same principles of light and shadow as a plain white box.

Sunlight and Shadow in Flowers

Up to this point, we have been talking about light and boxes, but how does this relate to flowers in the garden or in the vase? Flowers are a collection of graceful curves and rounded shapes—much more complex than a white box. Shadow sides, shade, cast shadows and crevice darks are everywhere within one bloom. But the same principles you just observed with the boxes also apply to flowers.

Color Temperature

As you probably suspect, curved surfaces facing the sun are warmest at the top of the curve and then cool as they turn from the light. Reflected color often affects only a portion of a petal, and cast shadows abound. Though these areas demand our observant attention, they are also what make flowers so beautiful.

Colorful Experiment

Why not try this experiment? On a sunny day, place a box outside so that one vertical side faces the light. Observe the color temperature differences on each surface. Next, try placing brightly colored paper adjacent to the shadow side of the box. Notice that reflected light is just that—light! To observe color temperature changes on a curved surface, use a can or look at a tree trunk in full sunlight. These changes are most obvious in the morning or evening hours. Once you become aware of varying color temperatures, you can apply this knowledge to everything you paint, including your florals.

In this photograph of the white magnolia blossoms, we can see all the aspects of color temperature and value.

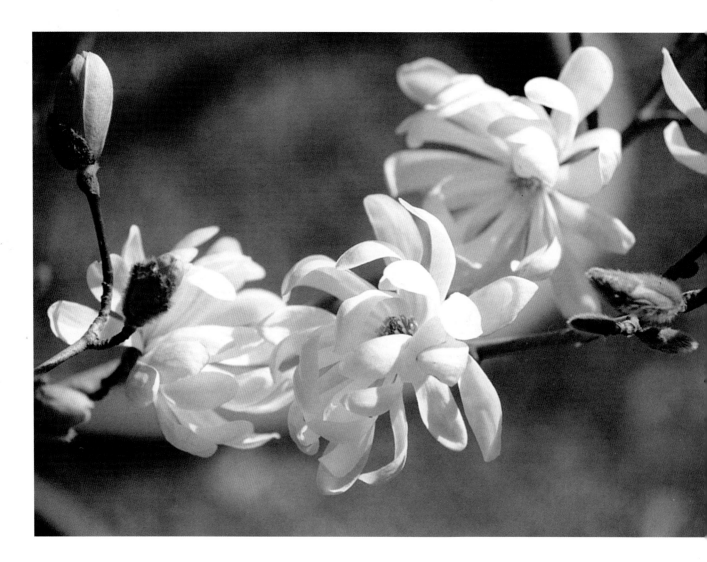

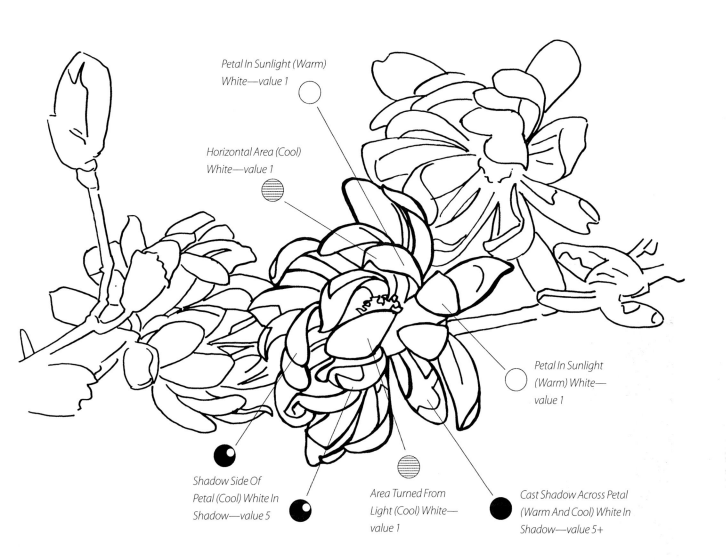

Petal In Sunlight (Warm) White—value 1

Horizontal Area (Cool) White—value 1

Petal In Sunlight (Warm) White— value 1

Shadow Side Of Petal (Cool) White In Shadow—value 5

Area Turned From Light (Cool) White— value 1

Cast Shadow Across Petal (Warm And Cool) White In Shadow—value 5+

Here is a line drawing of the magnolia blossoms. I've pointed out some areas of light and shadow, warm and cool color temperatures, and value scale numbers. Refer to the photo to see the actual color temperature and value differences.

Using Color Temperature

Let's paint a poppy using what we have learned about how the color of objects is affected by sunlight. I have drawn the poppy for you so we can concentrate on painting.

Materials

SURFACE
140-lb (300gsm) Arches cold-press watercolor paper

WATERCOLORS
Cobalt Blue, New Gamboge, Winsor Blue

BRUSHES
Nos. 6, 8 and 10 round

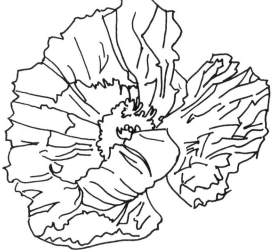

1 The Sketch
Sketch the poppy onto your watercolor paper.

2 Areas Facing the Sun
Study the drawing and paint a very pale wash of New Gamboge on the vertical surfaces that receive direct light. Notice I did not paint a solid yellow across these petals. Rather, the edges are a slightly deeper hue that quickly washes out to paper color.

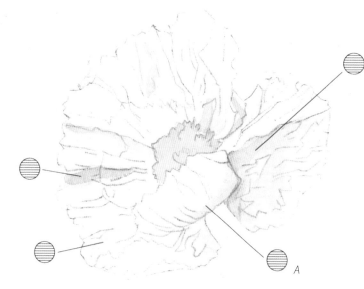

3 Areas Reflecting the Sky
Paint horizontal areas that reflect the sky, or petals that turn from the light with a pale wash of Cobalt Blue. Notice how, at first, petal A faces the light, then it turns, so the color temperature becomes cooler. The yellow center is painted last.

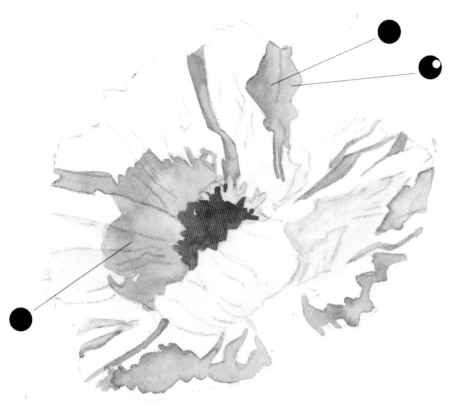

4 Cast Shadows and Shadow Sides

Mix a puddle of Cobalt Blue with a touch of Winsor Blue and test it to be sure it is value 4 or 5 when dry. Once you are satisfied, paint the shadow shapes. Your brush should hold enough pigment to paint the entire shadow area. While the paint is still wet, "charge in" New Gamboge and Rose Madder where you want to suggest reflected light. I know the color won't go exactly where you planned, but resist the temptation to make corrections. Everything will take its place in the next step. To go back is to invite trouble.

Decide on the value of the yellow center and paint the shadow four values darker.

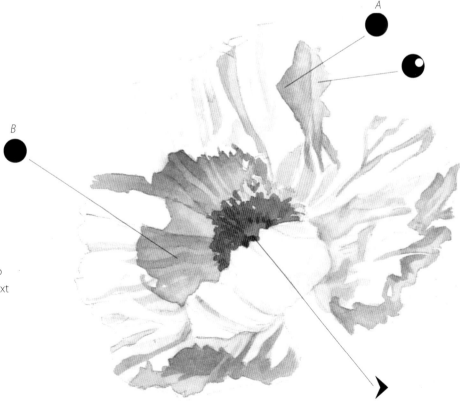

5 Final Modeling, Darks and Detail

Use a mid-value Cobalt Blue to model the shapes that give the wrinkled appearance to the poppy. You can use the same blue to model shapes within the shadow areas. Next darken the cast shadows where required (areas A and B).

The final step is to suggest the stigma with the addition of crevice darks in the center of the flower.

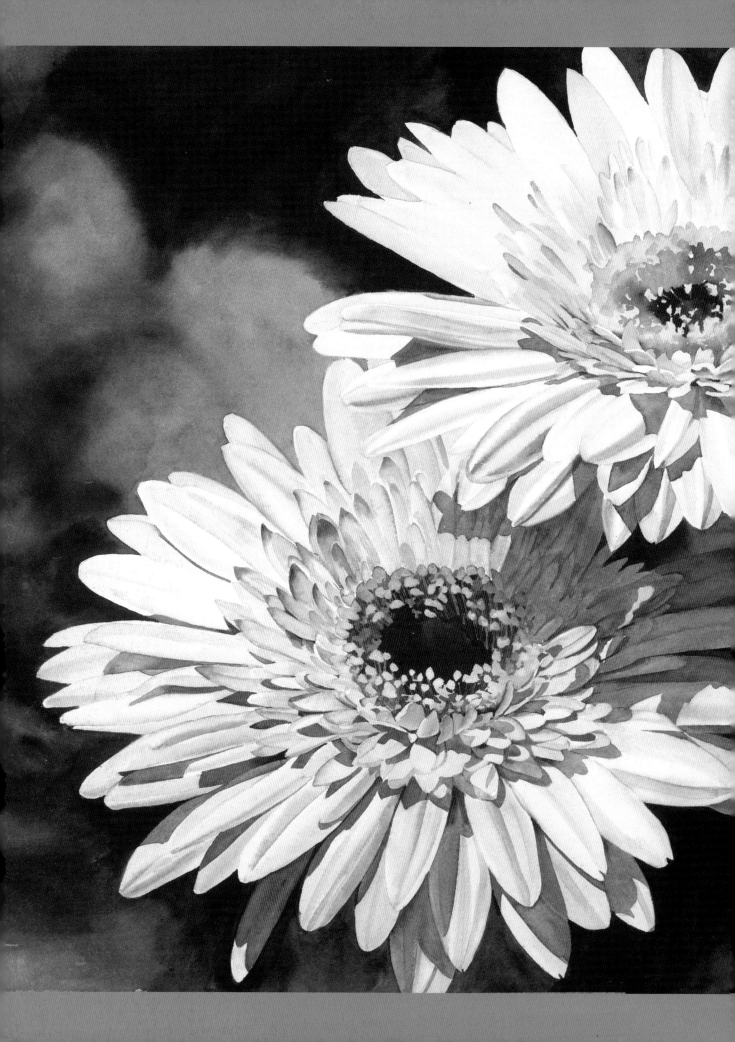

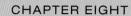
8

Reference of Essential Floral Painting Techniques

The purpose of this chapter is to provide you with easily accessible reference for handling many of the recurring elements you will encounter in floral painting with watercolor.

Before we get into some of the special techniques for flower painting, I want to cover a few areas that beginning and even experienced watercolor painters sometimes have trouble with: using enough water, and dealing with run-backs, or balloons.

Sunny Side Up
20" × 26" (51cm × 66cm)

How Much Water?

Learning how much water it takes to create the effect you want is basic to successful watercolor painting. Getting it right takes practice. Most of the beginning painters I know don't use enough water. So, if you are having a problem, perhaps you need more water on your brush.

Scale of Wetness

In the demonstrations that follow, I will refer to the following terms:

- *Dampen:* Wet the paper so it has absorbed some water but is not saturated.
- *Moisten:* Wet it so it has absorbed all the water it can hold.
- *Wet:* The paper is beyond saturation and the surface glistens in the light.
- *Puddle:* The water stands on the surface and will run if you tip the paper.

Fully Loaded

We need one more definition here. Oftentimes I will say the brush should be *fully loaded*. To be fully loaded, the whole brush, not just the tip, is made to hold all the water it can without dripping.

The sketches below illustrate how to prepare a fully loaded brush. Remember, the size of the brush you use should always be determined by the size of the area you intend to paint. Just because you need a fully loaded brush doesn't necessarily mean you need a large one. Generally, a fully loaded brush is used on dry paper.

When you paint with a fully loaded brush, you will make a puddle of color on the paper. The advantage is that you will be able to control the edges and move the color around freely. This puddle of color also gives you the opportunity to "charge" colors into the wet surface.

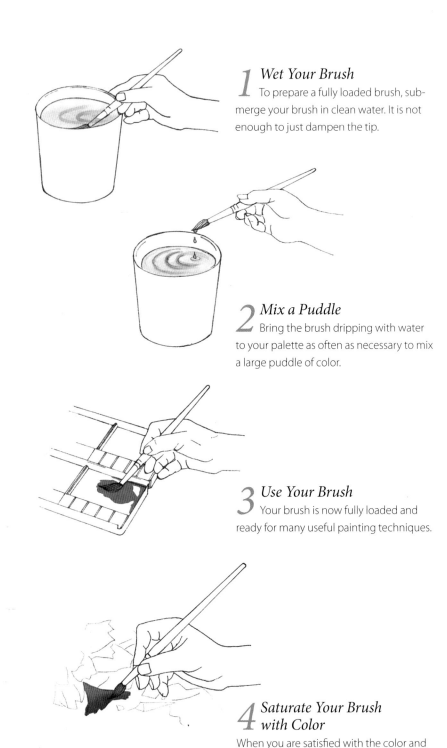

1 Wet Your Brush
To prepare a fully loaded brush, submerge your brush in clean water. It is not enough to just dampen the tip.

2 Mix a Puddle
Bring the brush dripping with water to your palette as often as necessary to mix a large puddle of color.

3 Use Your Brush
Your brush is now fully loaded and ready for many useful painting techniques.

4 Saturate Your Brush with Color
When you are satisfied with the color and value, completely saturate the bristles of your brush. Once loaded, you may want to tap the brush onto your palette to prevent dripping, but do not use your paint rag.

Run-Backs or Balloons

Many students ask me about run-backs, or balloons. Run-backs happen whenever wet pigment (or water) is added to a surface that has begun to dry. Or perhaps an area you've painted has developed a puddle near the edge, leaving part of the passage considerably wetter than the rest. Left to dry unattended, the moisture could seep back into the drying surface and create a run-back.

If you use a hair dryer to speed drying time, be careful to hold it back far enough to dry the surface uniformly.

It is sometimes possible to correct run-backs. Once the surface is thoroughly dry, use your regular brush to paint over the passage with clear water. This is often enough to "lift" the offending pigment and distribute it evenly. If the whole area you are painting is uniformly wet, the color will blend smoothly.

Run-backs happen when moisture is added to a surface that has begun to dry (top), or when a puddle is left to run back into a drying surface (bottom). Try to keep the painting surface uniformly wet.

Charging Color

Watercolor is unique in its ability to blend from one hue to the next in a cascade of flowing color. Learning to control and direct this marvelous medium is what keeps watercolorists fascinated (and confounded).

At some time, most of us have added pigment to a wet passage and watched the colors blend. Charging color, as described here is a slightly different technique. In this exercise, we will begin with one color on our brush and add different colors as we cover more of the dry surface.

Almost everything you do in watercolor is dependent on mastering these wet-into-wet skills. You need to charge color to make a petal appear to bend, to add a variety of color to a background, or to introduce reflected light to a shadow side. In these sketches and in those to follow, you will see that charging color is basic to painting watercolor florals.

Our subject here is one of the magnolias taken from the photograph and drawing on pages 78 and 79. The basic shape of this blossom is a sphere. The final painting must maintain this spherical shape.

Materials list

SURFACE
140-lb (300 gsm) Arches cold pressed watercolor paper

WATERCOLOR
Cobalt Blue, New Gamboge, Rose Madder Genuine

BRUSHES
Nos. 8 and 10 round

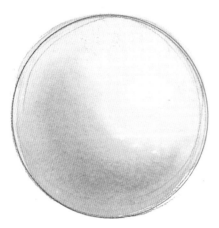

1 Study the Petals
The basic form of this blossom is a sphere. Study the individual petals on page 78 and 79 to help you understand how all of them are painted.

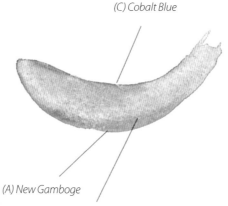
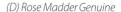

(C) Cobalt Blue

(D) Rose Madder Genuine

(A) New Gamboge

(B) Rose Madder Genuine

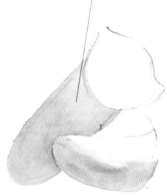

2 Paint a Puddle
With a fully loaded brush, paint a puddle of New Gamboge along the edge of the petal on the left (A). Next, add a fully loaded brush of Rose Madder Genuine next to the yellow puddle. Now let the colors blend (B). Use a fully loaded brush of Cobalt Blue along the top edge (C). Now, ease off. If the puddle is unmanageable, use a clean, thirsty brush to carefully pick up excess water along the side, but do not go back to correct the color. In this small space, the colors will stay more or less where you put them.

3 Continue Puddling
Use the same technique on the next two petals. The larger petal receives a long passage of rose madder genuine to suggest light penetrating through the overlapping petal (D).

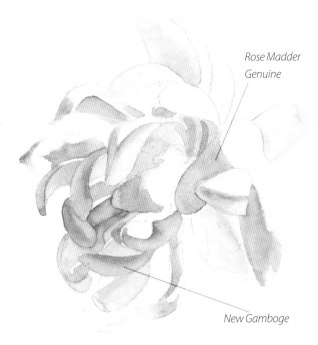

Rose Madder
Genuine

New Gamboge

5 *Final*

The final painting should maintain the spherical shape of the blossom.

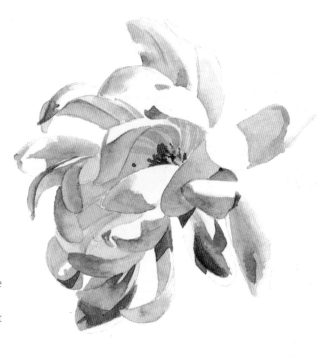

4 *Develop the Blossoms*

Continue with this technique to develop the blossoms you see here. Notice how all the petals on the blossom possess the same overall shadow pattern that matches the original sphere shape. Cast shadows and details are added to complete the sketch.

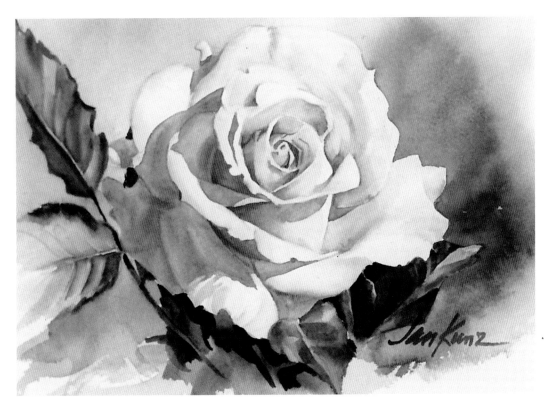

CHARGING COLOR EXAMPLE

I charged color into the shadow side of these petals to suggest reflected light and to suggest the illusion of roundness. I also charged color into the background for greater depth and interest. Additional colors used here include Burnt Sienna and Sap Green.

Mary's Rose
8"x 10" (20cm x 25cm)

Sunlight and Shadow in Flowers

There may be times when you want to suggest the presence of foliage in the background. To accomplish this, I begin with a charged wash. Once that's dry, I look for color and value changes in the wash to suggest emerging shapes. It takes a bit of imagination, but as you can see from the sketch below, foliage shapes can be discovered and developed easily from a charged wash. This technique is useful when painting other subjects as well. In my painting *Sunday Afternoon*, many of the flowers behind the central figures were developed by painting around discovered floral shapes in the background wash. The same technique was used to create a bower of leaves behind the girls' heads in *The Sisters*.

Blending Colors

Heavier Pigment

To suggest background foliage, begin with a charged wash. Look for places where some of the pigment is heavier, or where colors blend.

Use light values of Cobalt Blue or Winsor Blue to reinforce some of the emerging shapes.

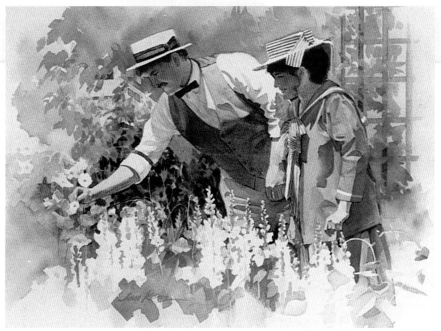

Sunday Afternoon
22" × 30" (56cm × 76cm)

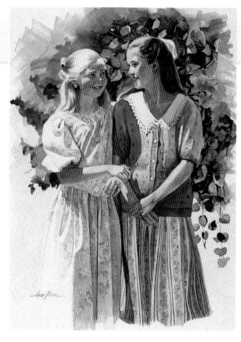

The Sisters
30" × 22" (76cm × 56cm)

"Discovered" floral and foliage shapes surround the central figures in both these paintings.

Add a darker color to make new shapes within and around the shapes you have outlined.

Continue developing leaves and stems until you have achieved the desired effect.

Painting Lush Greens

When colors blend on the paper (rather than in the palette), the resulting mixture is brilliant and creates movement. Experiment by painting puddles of various yellows, blues and greens, permitting them to blend on the paper. You will discover a wide variety of intriguing greens. Don't forget to charge in a few warm colors. You may want to suggest places where the leaves have been burned by the sun or have begun to change color.

Keep in mind, unless you are making a poster, it is never a good idea to use just one color to describe the leaves and stems in your painting.

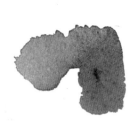

Viridian Green + Cadmium Orange

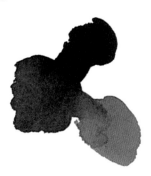

Winsor Blue + Winsor Green

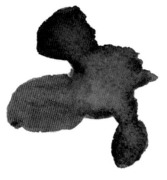

Raw Sienna + Winsor Green + Winsor Blue

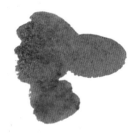

Cobalt Blue + Viridian Green

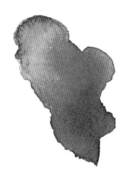

Sap Green + Cadmium Orange

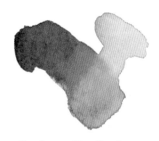

Sap Green + New Gamboge

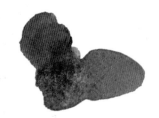

Raw Sienna + Viridian Green

Alizarin Crimson + Sap Green

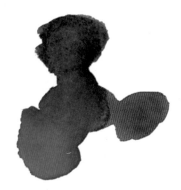

*Winsor Green + Turquoise Blue
+ Cadmium Orange*

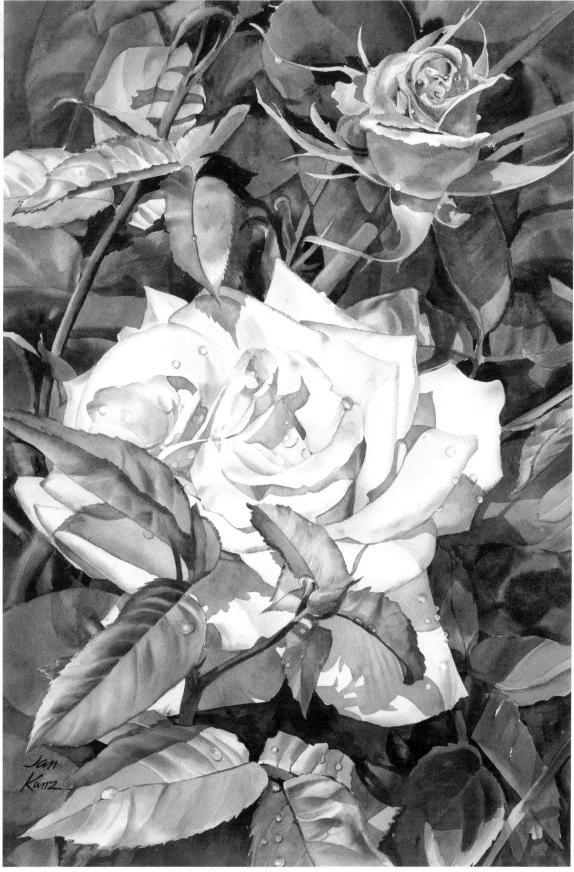

Peace Rose
30" × 19" (76cm × 48cm)

How boring this painting would be if I had used only one color of green, right from the tube, to paint the background stems and leaves. As it is, there are dozens of colors—both warm and cool—making up the overall green of the rose leaves.

Curled Edges Receiving Reflected Light

Many petals and leaves have curled edges and depicting them presents a wonderful opportunity to add color and brilliance to your floral painting. We can achieve the illusion of curled edges by remembering that surfaces become cooler in color temperature as they turn from the light. Frequently, curled edges also receive reflected light from an adjacent petal.

In this illustration, the petals of the rose curve in many directions, but the painting process is very much the same for all of the petals. Let's take a closer look at the petals in the boxed area. At right are three stages of development. I have exaggerated the color and shadow shapes to help you see how they were painted.

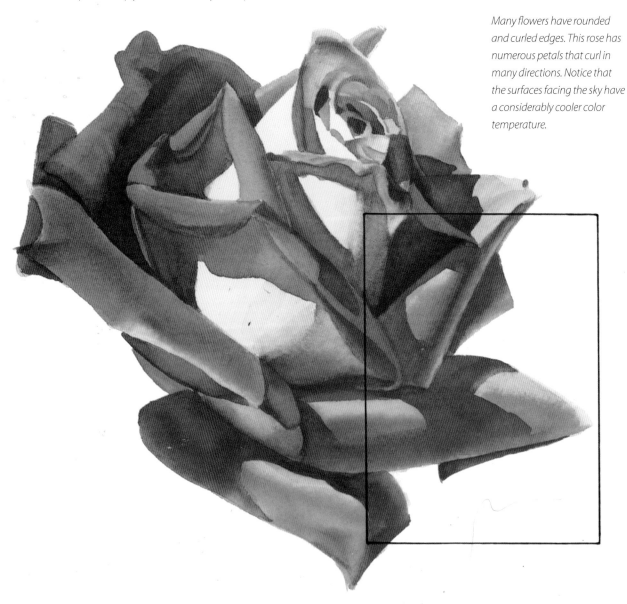

Many flowers have rounded and curled edges. This rose has numerous petals that curl in many directions. Notice that the surfaces facing the sky have a considerably cooler color temperature.

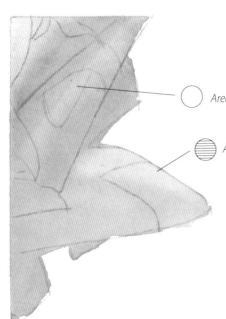

1 Paint Local Color
Adjust color temperature to reflect horizontal and vertical surfaces. Let it dry.

○ *Area facing sun*

⊖ *Area facing sky*

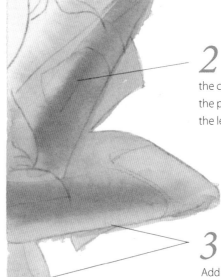

2 Reflected Light
If necessary, reinstate color on the curved surface by first wetting the petal and dashing in color along the length of the curve. Let it dry.

3 Complete One Petal at a Time
Add color along the entire shadow edge receiving reflected light. Keep it wet!

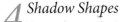

4 Shadow Shapes
Have colors ready and know the boundaries of the shadow shapes before you begin! You will find it easier to work one petal at a time.

5 Add Shadow Color
Alongside the brilliant yellow passage, add shadow color and permit the colors to flow together. Complete the shadow. Let it dry before you begin the next petal.

Painting Around Complex Edges

A large background can be painted a portion at a time and still look as if it were completed in a single spectacular wash. You can paint as far as you feel you have control of the medium, stop, let it dry, and then begin again. The trick is to keep the overlapping edges soft.

This technique is especially valuable when you paint around the complex shapes of blossoms. Plan ahead and have a place to stop before the paint begins to dry. Remember, painting an area that has begun to dry is what causes run-backs.

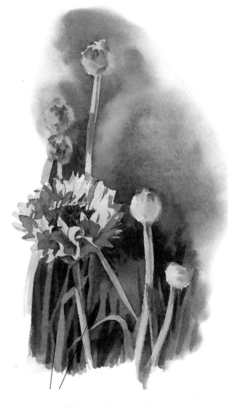

2 Paint Around the Petals

Before painting around the petals, prepare a place to stop by wetting with clear water an area at a comfortable distance.

Working on dry paper, paint around the petals with the background colors. Stop at the wet boundary you have prepared and permit the colors to flow into it.

1 Paint Flowers and Stems

Paint the flowers and stems first and let dry. Next, paint small areas between the stems and permit to dry.

3 Complete the Background

Make ever-widening circles of color until the background is complete. Be sure to make the pre-wet area wet enough and wide enough (at least ¼" [6mm]) to prevent a hard edge.

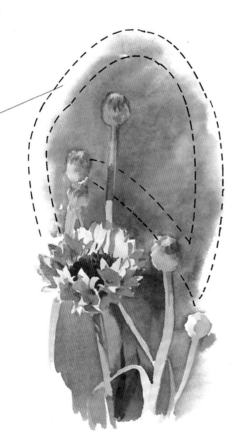

4 Add Final Details

Add any details after the surface is dry.

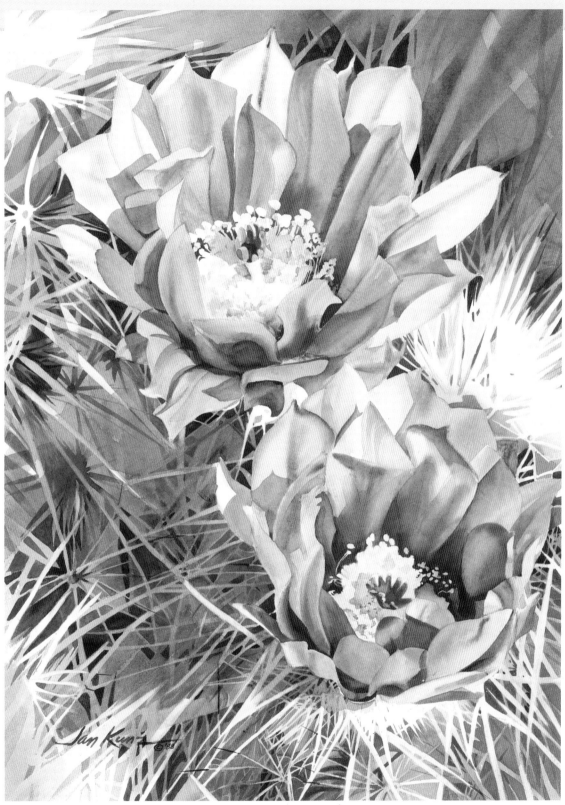

Cactus Flower
30" × 19" (76cm × 48cm)

The cactus spikes provided natural stopping places for the background color, thus giving me ample time to carefully paint around the cactus flower's petal. In some places, I painted to a straight edge, leaving a white spike. Places where background colors overlapped were concealed with the addition of a darker spike. Still other spikes were lifted with the use of an acetate frisket (see Chapter 1). I did not use liquid frisket in this painting.

Cast Shadows

We have already seen how dark cast shadows must be to represent a sunny day (Chapter 7). Not only should they be the correct value and logically placed, but they should suggest the shape of the object that cast them.

Cast shadows, like reflected light, offer an opportunity for color and interest. Since our eyes are accustomed to making the comparison between the edge of the shadow and the sunstruck surface, we think of shadows as cold and dark.

We can add interest to shadow shapes if we take advantage of this phenomenon by painting the shadow's edges a cooler hue.

But fill the rest of the cast shadow with lots of color. Use color in the same value range, and usually from the same side of the color wheel. However, a warm touch in a cool shadow also works well.

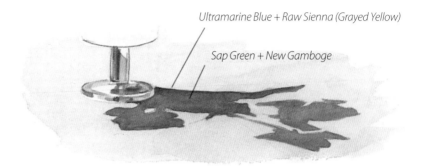

Ultramarine Blue + Raw Sienna (Grayed Yellow)

Sap Green + New Gamboge

Shadows appear colder where they meet the sunlit area. Often, cast shadows begin with a hard edge, and then become less distinct as the shadow lengthens.

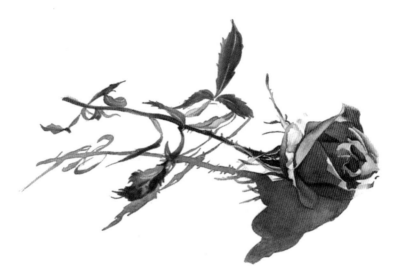

In this painting of a rose, accurate placement of the shadow required great care. To represent sunlight, the cast shadow must be the same hue and 40 percent-plus darker than the object upon which it is cast. In this sketch (as in the one above), the leading edge of the shadow is slightly cooler in color temperature than the body of the shadow shape.

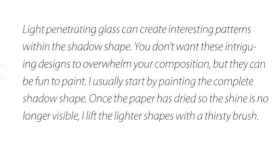

Light penetrating glass can create interesting patterns within the shadow shape. You don't want these intriguing designs to overwhelm your composition, but they can be fun to paint. I usually start by painting the complete shadow shape. Once the paper has dried so the shine is no longer visible, I lift the lighter shapes with a thirsty brush.

Cluster Blooms

Several varieties of flowers, such as hydrangeas and lilacs, consist of clusters of hundreds of individual blossoms. Even if it were possible to render each little blossom, the overall effect might be considerably less than desirable.

The solution I favor is to determine the shape of the overall cluster and paint it first.

After the basic form is complete, suggest individual blooms, making sure that the shape of the original cluster is preserved.

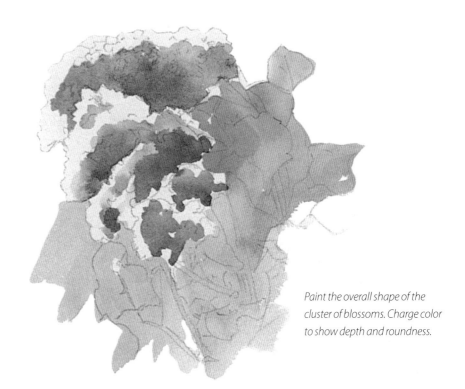

Paint the overall shape of the cluster of blossoms. Charge color to show depth and roundness.

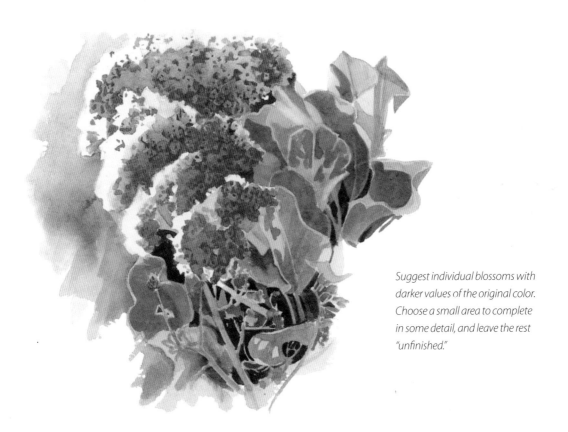

Suggest individual blossoms with darker values of the original color. Choose a small area to complete in some detail, and leave the rest "unfinished."

Glazing to Create a Distance

Glazing is one way to "set" one flower (or passage) in front of another. I generally use a pale wash of Cobalt Blue for this purpose. In light values, Cobalt Blue will form a light haze without destroying the color integrity of the background area.

Other pigments you may consider for this purpose are those that contain no black. Rose Madder, Cobalt Violet and Ultramarine Blue (in very light values) are three of my favorites. You may find it helpful to experiment before you run the wash!

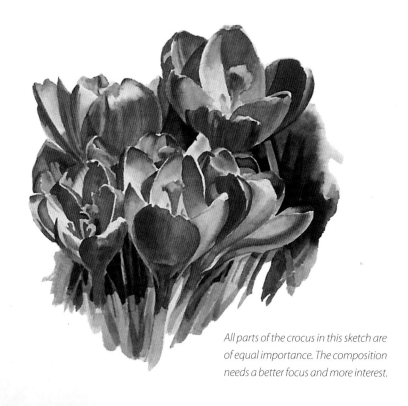

All parts of the crocus in this sketch are of equal importance. The composition needs a better focus and more interest.

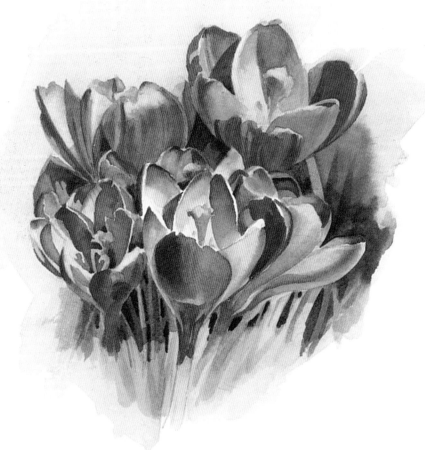

In this illustration, all but the central bloom has been "pushed back." This illusion was accomplished by painting over the background flowers and around the central blossom with a wash of Cobalt Blue. A different effect can be achieved by beginning with a very light valued glaze and adding successively darker glazes as the flowers diminish in importance.

Convex and Concave Curves

Both convex and concave shapes are often found on the same flower. These curved shapes may be suggested in many ways. One of the best ways to increase the illusion of a curved surface is by cooling the color temperature of an area as it turns from the light.

In this illustration, I used the shape of the petals and the shape of the shadows, as well as the placement of reflected light, to create the illusion of concave and convex surfaces.

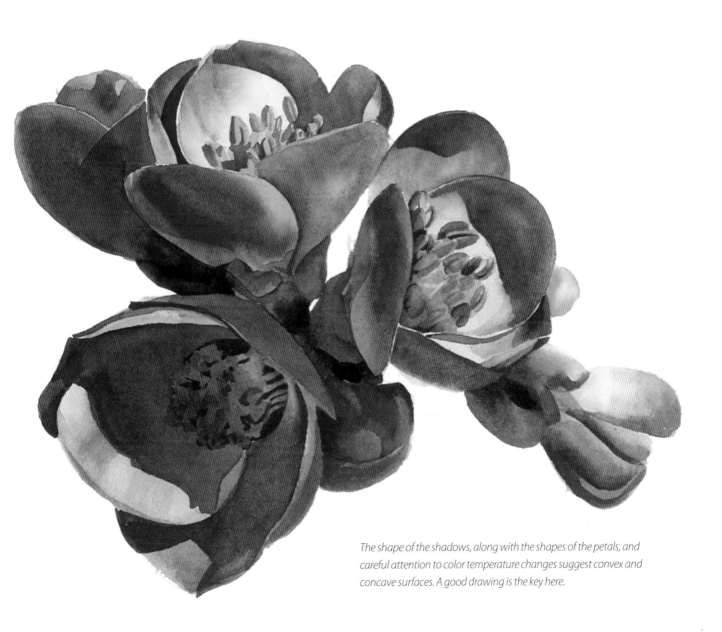

The shape of the shadows, along with the shapes of the petals, and careful attention to color temperature changes suggest convex and concave surfaces. A good drawing is the key here.

Suggesting Form with Line

Line is still another way to suggest surface form. The iris petal appears to curve back, largely because of the vein lines on its surface. A change in color temperature further enforces the illusion. As with everything you paint, observation is the key.

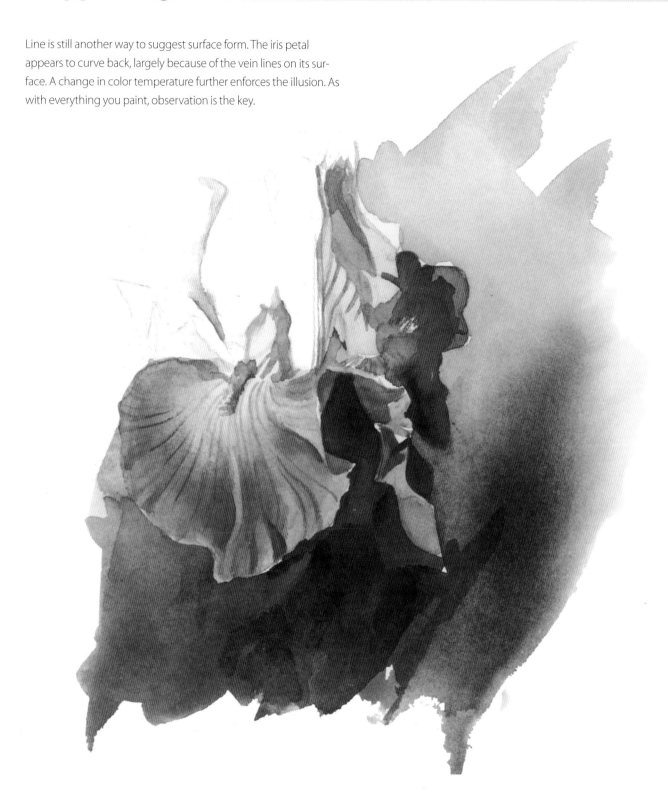

Line and color temperature can help to suggest curving forms. On this iris, the vein lines, added to the value and color changes, strongly indicate the form of the petals.

Painting Folds and Ruffles

There are several things to keep in mind when painting multi-ruffled blooms. Not only is the whole flower subject to sun and shadow, but every ruffle and fold moves from direct sun to shade, and then into shadow, many times within one petal. The value changes have to be consistent! There are many opportunities to introduce reflected light.

It's easier than you may think to become so intrigued painting a flower's ruffles and folds that you lose sight of its overall shape. Study your subject carefully. Draw the shadow and highlight shapes. You will probably need to simplify them considerably.

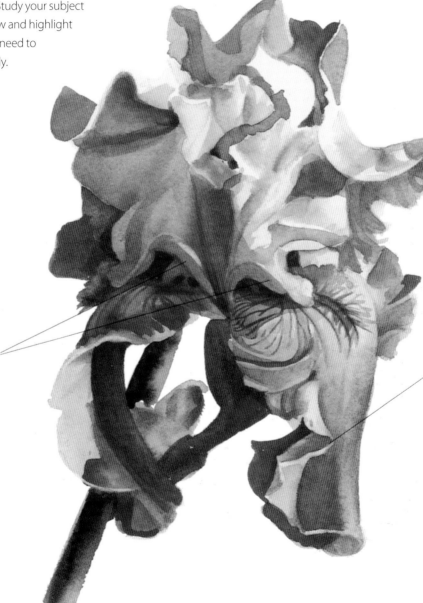

With careful observation, you'll find many opportunities to introduce reflected light. These small areas add more than you would think to the beauty, and the believability, of your painting.

Every petal has dimension: Each has a part facing the light, another facing the sky, and still another in shadow, as well as many areas of reflected light and cast shadows.

Painting Leaves

Materials list

WATERCOLORS
New Gamboge

Sap Green

Burnt Sienna

Leaves are beautiful and deserve a careful look. Most of the leaves you encounter will not be as complicated as the leaf in this illustration. However, leaves that have a prominent place in the floral arrangement should be rendered with as much care as the blossoms themselves.

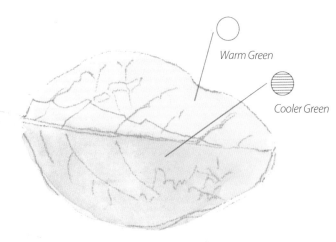

Warm Green

Cooler Green

1 Add interest and color to leaves by considering first their relationship to the source of light, and using differences in color temperature as a foundation to build on.

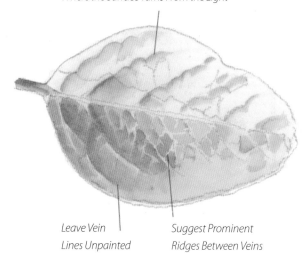

Moisten Along the Vein Line and Add Color to Suggest Where the Surface Turns From the Light

Leave Vein Lines Unpainted

Suggest Prominent Ridges Between Veins

2 Add the cast shadows, keeping a harder, cooler edge on the sunlit side and a softer edge on the shadow side.

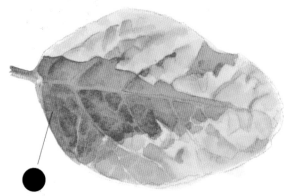

Add Cast Shadows

3 Add the last shadow.

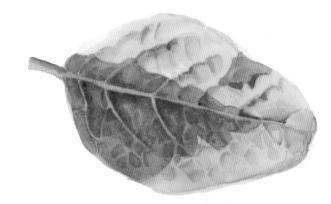

4 Reinforce color where required and make final corrections. I added some more of the cooler green to the bottom half to retrieve the warm/cool division I set up in the first step. I also developed some of the unique contours of the leaf and darkened some areas along the vein lines to show them more distinctly.

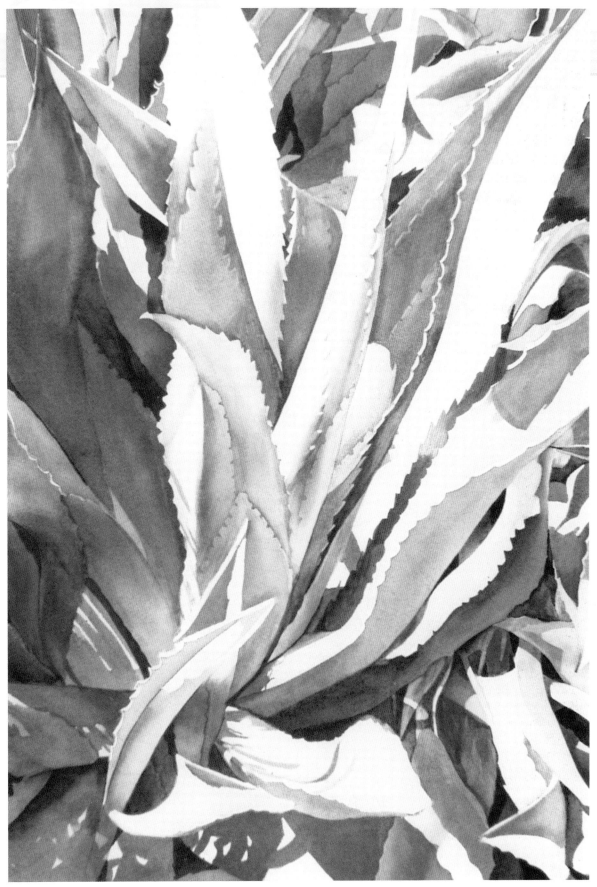

Century Plant
30" × 22" (76cm × 56cm)

Leaves are beautiful and deserve a careful look. Most of the leaves you encounter will not be as compli-
cated as the leaf in this illustration. However, leaves that have a prominent place in the floral arrangement
should be rendered with as much care as the blossoms themselves.

Dewdrops

Dewdrops are fun and easy to paint. They can add sparkle, but use them sparingly. Note that dewdrops always take on the hue of what they are sitting on.

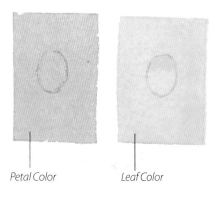

Petal Color   *Leaf Color*

1 *Draw the Dewdrop*
Draw the dewdrop into position. Wet the spot carefully, almost to the point of creating a puddle.

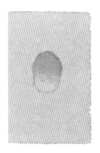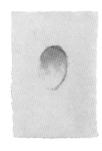

2 *Place a Darker-Value Drop*
Use a fairly dry brush and a darker-value drop of the petal (or leaf) color into the part of the dewdrop that will face the light. Tip the paper if necessary to keep the color darkest near that end. Let it dry.

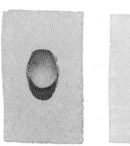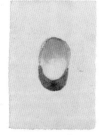

3 *Paint the Cast Shadow*
Paint in the cast shadow color at the other end of the drop shape.

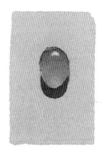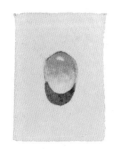

4 *Lift a Highlight*
Use a frisket or knife to lift a rounded highlight at the drop's sunlit end.

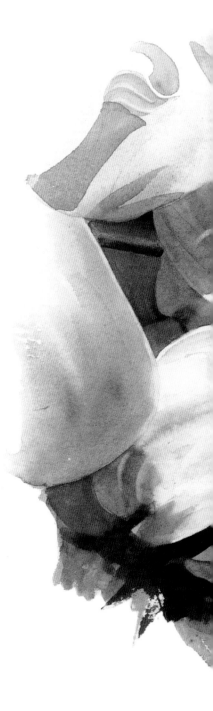

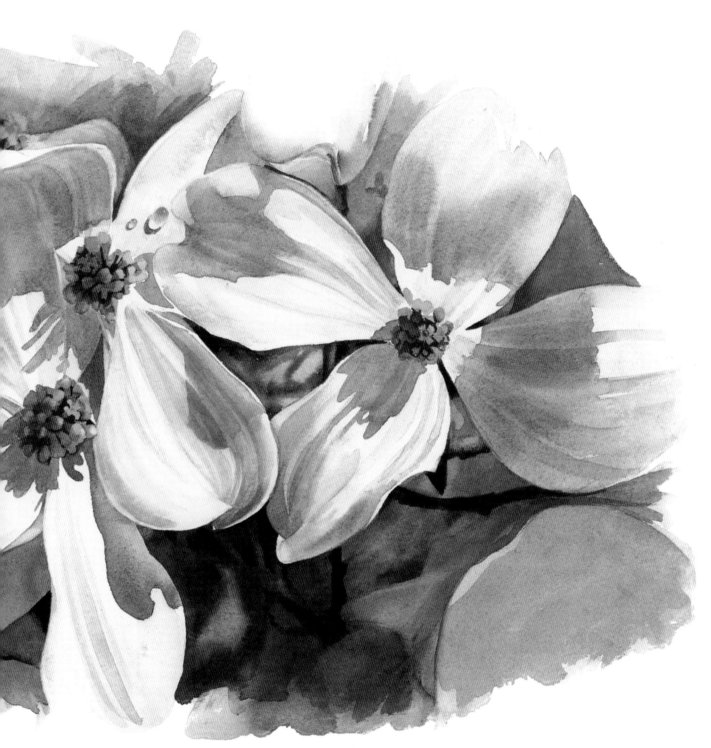

Be careful that the dewdrops you paint have their shadow and sunny sides aligned in accordance with the rest of the painting.

Puddle and Pull

You may find this "puddle and pull" brushstroke as useful as I do when painting pointed leaves and petals.

1 *Apply the Petal Tip*

Use a fully loaded brush to apply color to the tip of the petal you intend to paint. The pigment should form a small puddle. For this exercise, you can use whatever color you have in the brush.

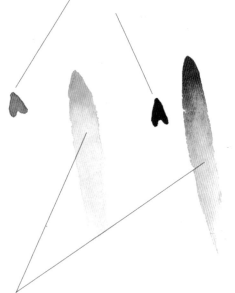

2 *Pull the Color Down*

Wash out your brush in clear water. Once clean, touch your brush to the paint rag, but permit a moderate amount of water to remain.

Begin the stroke at the bottom of the wet arrow shape, and pull the color down, leaving an ever lighter track.

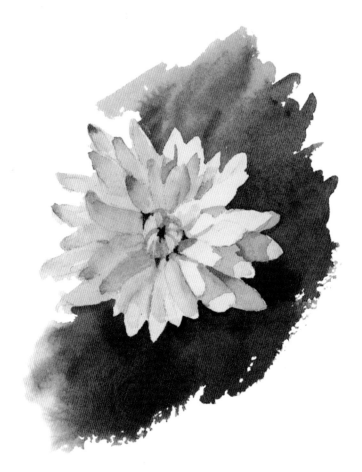

3 *Finish*

Let dry before going on to the next petal. Try this stroke when you paint pointed petals.

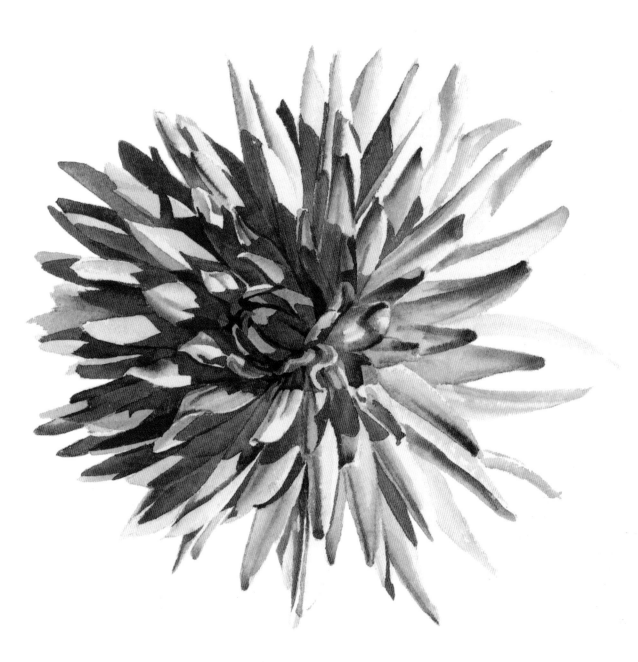

Puddle and pull brushstrokes were used to paint many of the spearlike petals on this watercolor sketch of a dahlia. This simple brushstroke can make complicated flowers much easier to paint.

Transparent Surfaces

Glass vases and jars may appear difficult to paint, but they can be surprisingly easy. The trick is to think of the shapes you see within the vase or jar as just that: a collection of shapes that you can paint one at a time.

The cut crystal vase on the next page appears more complicated than this plain glass vase, but the painting method is the same.

Materials list

WATERCOLORS

Cobalt Blue

New Gamboge

Sap Green

Burnt Sienna

Alizarin Crimson

Ultramarine Blue

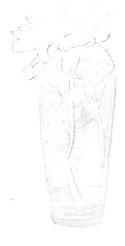

1 Paint the Lightest Values

Study the vase and look for color in the water. Work on a dry surface and paint in the lightest values, letting the colors flood together. Let them dry.

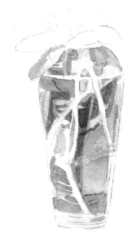

2 Paint the Darker Values

Look for darker shapes within the vase. Use the darker values and colors you see, and paint them freely. Here I painted around the stems because their sunstruck side is lighter than the background. If the stems had been darker, I would not have avoided them.

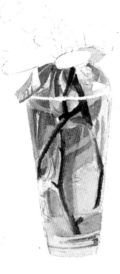

3 Add Foliage

Now it is time to add the stems and leaves within the vase. As you can see, I have tried to be fairly careful with these shapes.

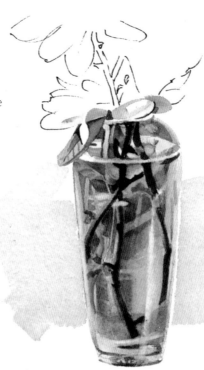

4 Lift the Highlights

Mix a light-value puddle of Cobalt Blue. Use a clean brush and a light touch to paint over the entire vase adding more color on the shadow side. Let it dry.

Finally, lift highlights with clean water and a stiff brush. Be sure the highlights follow the contour of the vase.

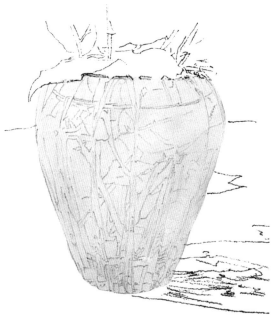

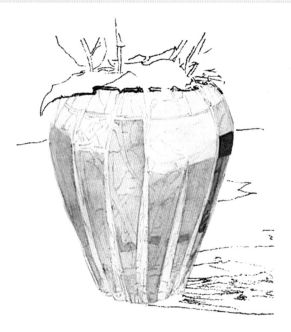

1 Begin with Blue

Working with a fully loaded brush, begin on the left side of the vase with a pale passage of Winsor Blue. Warm the color with Ultramarine Blue as you approach the other side.

2 Focus on the Faceted Surfaces

This vase is divided into faceted surfaces, providing natural stopping places. Concentrate on reproducing the color and value of each section, using various blues with touches of Rose Madder.

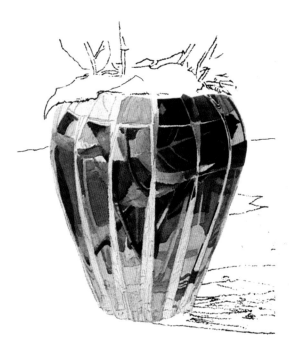

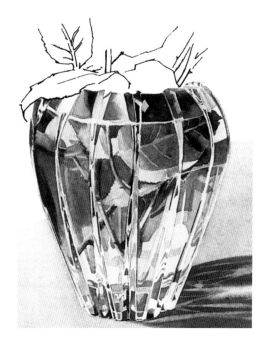

3 Suggest Shapes

Working a section at a time, begin to suggest leaf and stem shapes, now and then making them extend from one area to the next.

4 Add Dark Accents

Finally, add the dark accents along the edges of the faceted surfaces. The cast shadow comes last. Light streaking through the glass creates soft-edged designs in the shadow area. This illusion can be created by lifting pigment from the previously painted shadow.

Reflective Surfaces

I think successful painting is largely dependent on training your eye to see. You need to turn off your conscious brain and paint the shapes you see before you. The shapes in reflective surfaces may not make sense, but they define the surface of the object you are painting. You can do it, and it's fun!

Materials list

WATERCOLORS

New Gamboge

Alizarin Crimson

Cobalt Blue

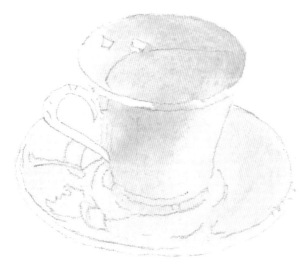

1 *Sketch and Wash*

Carefully draw the cup, and include any shapes you may see. This teacup is cream colored. The vertical side facing the light is toward yellow, but the horizontal surface of the saucer is more toward green. Let these first washes dry.

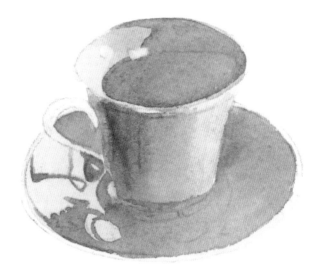

2 *Add the Shadows*

The shadow shapes are four values darker than the sunny side. They may possess strange shapes, but be as accurate as you can. Make them appear to follow the contour of the surface. Notice that the interior of the cup receives reflected light from the opposite side.

3 *Add the Extras*

Now for the fun part. Paint the extra squiggles you see within the large shadow shapes. Add the gold trim using Burnt Sienna, New Gamboge and Alizarin Crimson.

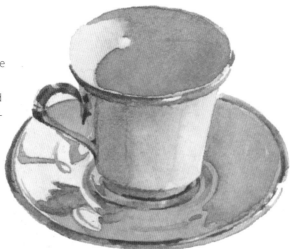

Backlighting

Backlighting can make a dramatic and exciting painting. One of the best ways to depict backlighting is to make the petals appear translucent, revealing the light that must be coming from behind them. It may take an object between the flower and the light to complete the illusion. With light from behind, petals appear darker where they intersect, or where a stem or leaf is blocking the direct light. The places where the translucent petals overlap may be slightly lighter than where the foliage blocks the sun.

In this illustration, light appears to penetrate one of the petals (A) and cast a glow across the shadow area. This illusion was created by painting the shadow side of the petal (receiving the sun) a warmer color than the rest of the shadow. After everything was dry, I glazed yellow over the cool shadow areas to suggest the glow.

Materials list

WATERCOLORS

Cobalt Blue

Alizarin Crimson

New Gamboge

Ultramarine Blue

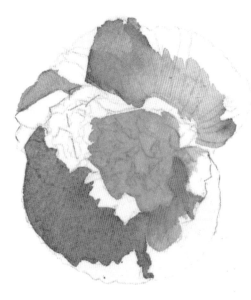

1 Paint the Cast Shadows
The cast shadows were painted freely; a few whites show sunstruck areas. The backlighted petal was painted a slightly lighter value and a warmer hue than the rest of the shadow area.

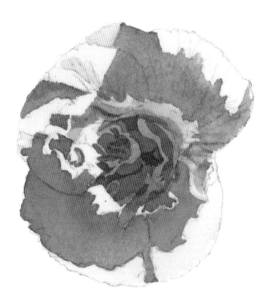

2 Discover Center Shapes
Smaller petal shapes in the center were discovered through the same technique described in the demonstration on pages 88 and 89.

3 Add the Darks and Details
Darks and details were added last. To paint the red borders, I began by painting a strip of clear water around the petal's edges and followed it quickly with a thin line of red pigment. The soft borders were created by letting the pigment flow into the wet surface. A backlit flower will usually appear more dark than light. Most of the lighter areas will be at the outside, thin parts of the petals. Many times a darker border will be visible at the edge, as seen here in red.

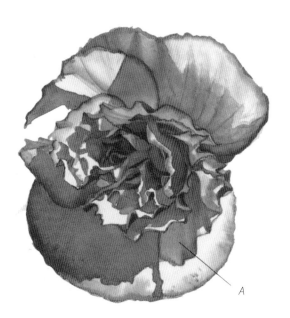

A

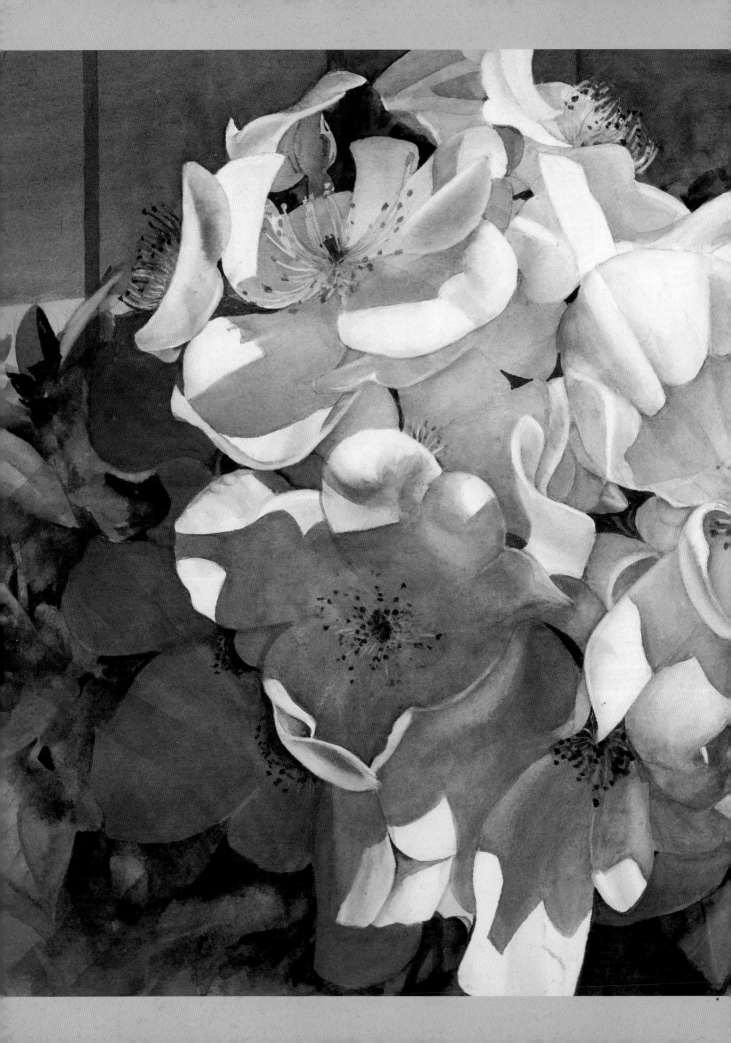

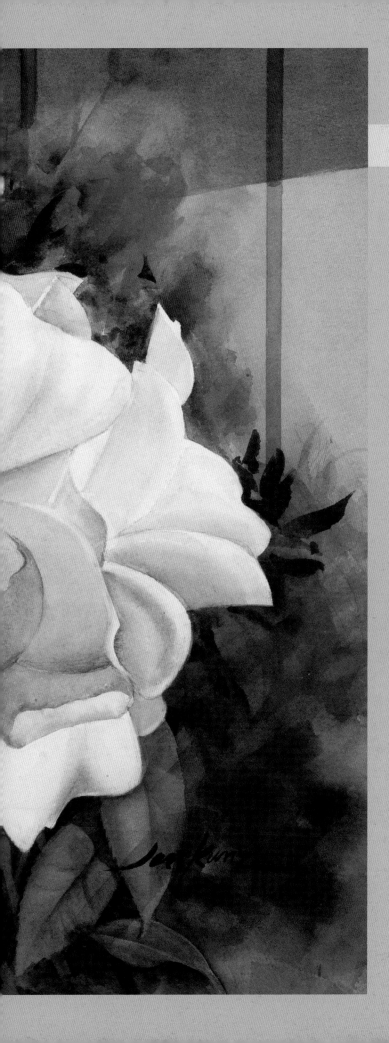

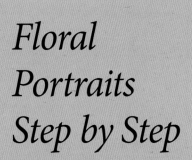

CHAPTER NINE

Floral Portraits Step by Step

Rather than simply show you the steps I go through toward making a finished floral portrait, I would now like to invite you to paint along with me. At the end of this chapter are all of the drawings I used in these demonstrations. You can trace over them, even enlarge them if you wish.

Before we begin to paint these floral portraits, I want to remind you to look first for the flowers' basic forms. As you modify these forms to suit the flower you are painting, think of shapes. The petals and leaves, as well as the planes and folds within them, are basically a variety of shapes.

You will discover that I don't begin every painting in the same way. Generally speaking, I like to work from light to dark. Just like you, I often have to feel my way and make decisions on instinct and experience. The more you paint, the more confidence you will have.

Backyard Roses
16" × 22" (41cm × 56cm)

Blue Iris

Making the Most of Local Color

In this demonstration, you will learn how to enhance a color with the addition of other related colors and still maintain the integrity of the original hue.

You may see places where you'll want to employ some of the special floral painting techniques described in Chapter 8. These will include:

- Curled edges receiving reflected light
- Painting convex and concave surfaces
- Painting folds and ruffles
- Painting around complex shapes

The size of the brush you use should be appropriate to the size of your painting. Often you have a favorite brush, and that is the one you need. This time we will paint directly on dry paper. We will work slowly and feel our way along until we gain confidence.

Materials

SURFACE
22" × 30" (56cm × 76cm) 300-lb. (640gsm) Arches cold-press water-color paper

WATERCOLORS
Alizarin Crimson, Burnt Sienna, Cadmium Red, Cobalt Blue, New Gamboge, Rose Madder Genuine, Turquoise Blue, Ultramarine Blue

BRUSHES
1-inch (25mm) flat

Nos. 6, 10, 14 and 26 round

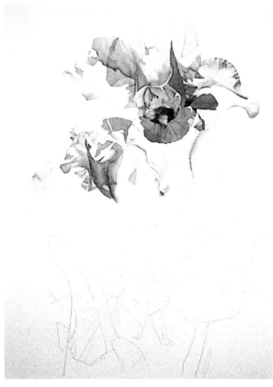

Step 1

1 Getting Started

Once the drawing is traced onto the watercolor paper, let's begin to develop the petal in the upper right.

Wet the lower portion of the petal with clear water. Now add a very pale yellow glow to the right side. Don't add this color across the whole petal, just a glow in the bottom corner to suggest direct sunlight. Let it dry.

To suggest the reflected light visible where the petal bends to become vertical, add New Gamboge along the length of the bend, and immediately add blue above it. Let the colors blend, then soften the top of the blue edge, and let it dry.

The ruffle at the top comes next. Wet the area. With very little water on your brush (because it's already on the paper), add Turquoise Blue, Winsor Blue and Ultramarine Blue. Add these colors one at a time, permitting some places to be darker than others to suggest texture.

The cast shadows are value 5 since the petal in sunlight is value 1. Use Winsor Blue and Turquoise Blue on the leading edge and Ultramarine Blue and Rose Madder to warm the colors near the center.

Work across the top petal, painting shapes as you see them. A confident brushstroke is important here—no matter if you make a few mistakes. You may be surprised at how good it looks!

Use the same colors and technique to finish this blossom and begin the next.

The anther in shadow is New Gamboge, Alizarin Crimson, Cadmium Red, Burnt Sienna and Burnt Umber at the center.

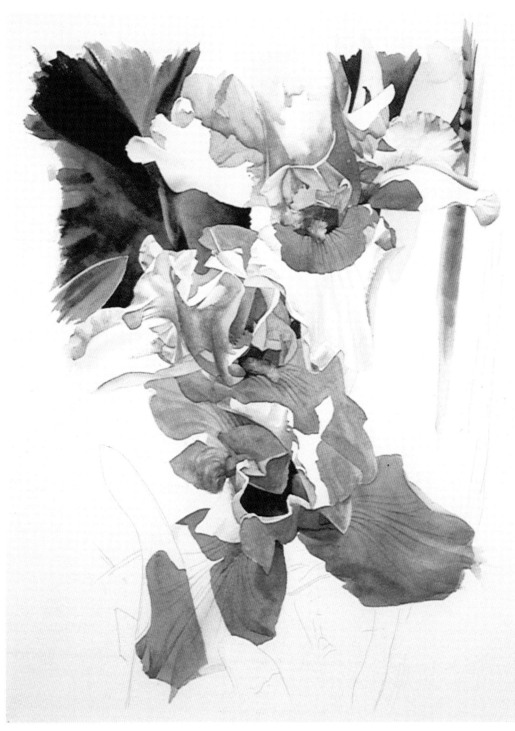

2 Working Across the Page

Continue painting one blossom at a time, using the technique described in Step 1. Remember to use a fully loaded brush and add colors, one at a time, permitting them to blend on the paper.

Begin the background. Use various combinations of blue, green and yellow. Work on one area at a time, painting carefully around the complex petal shapes. Use the technique described on page 94.

Step 2

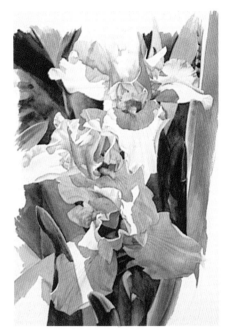

Step 3

3 Blending Background Colors

Irises are complex shapes, so we want to keep the background simple. Use dark colors close to one another in value. Begin with the medium values and add darker ones. As before, lay the colors next to one another and let them blend on the paper. No mixing in the palette or stroking them together. Keep the greatest contrast between the blossoms and the background.

4 Final Touches

After the painting is dry, develop the spear-shaped leaves, and add any remaining detail.

Once you are finished, survey your work. Ask yourself: Are the value relationships consistent? Have I been careful with the edges? Have I taken advantage of reflected light? What have I learned from this painting to help me on the next?

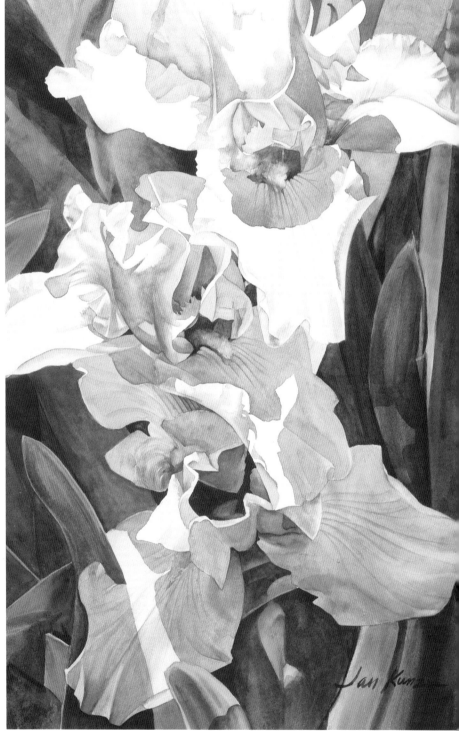

Step 4

Rhododendrons

Painting the Subject Your Way

The colors I used in this painting are New Gamboge, Rose Madder Genuine, Cobalt Blue, Burnt Sienna, Alizarin Crimson, Winsor Blue, Burnt Umber, Raw Umber, Winsor Green and Sap Green.

The painting method for backlighted petals on page 111 works equally well for backlighted leaves. The leaves themselves are shown on page 102.

I used no. 12 and no. 14 round brushes for the large leaves, and no. 6 and no. 8 for the petals. The dark red dots, as well as some small areas, were painted with a no. 4 round. I worked on a half sheet (15" × 22" [38 cm × 56 cm]) of cold press watercolor paper.

Materials

SURFACE
15" × 22" (38 cm × 56 cm) 300-lb. (640gsm) cold-press watercolor paper

BRUSHES
Nos. 4, 6, 8, 12, and 14 round

WATERCOLORS
New Gamboge, Rose Madder Genuine, Cobalt Blue, Burnt Sienna, Alizarin Crimson, Winsor Blue, Burnt Umber, Raw Umber, Winsor Green, Sap Green

OTHER TOOLS
Liquid frisket
Rubber cement
Pencil

Step 1

1 Apply Liquid Frisket

After the drawing is complete, begin by applying liquid frisket to protect the blossom's stamen. Start with New Gamboge along the bottom line of the central blossom's top petal (to suggest reflected light). Immediately add Rose Madder Genuine and Alizarin Crimson above the yellow passage and let the colors blend. Let it dry.

Next, paint right over the liquid frisket as you complete the blossom.

2 Determine Light Source

Before you paint the rest of the blossoms, ask yourself if the petal you are painting is facing the sun, turned from the light or in shadow. Check for value.

Use the dark red dots on the central petal to help suggest its curving surface. Begin by dampening (page 84) the petal with clear water. Now, lift a gob of fresh Alizarin Crimson with a small brush, and add the dots. Be careful to position them correctly.

Once a blossom is completed and dried, remove the liquid frisket. I use a rubber cement pick-up for this purpose, but an eraser will do.

Paint the small, pointed unformed blossoms at the left of the central bloom by charging various combinations of red, yellow, green and blue onto a dry surface.

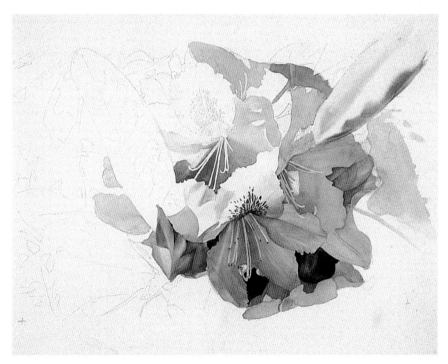

Step 2

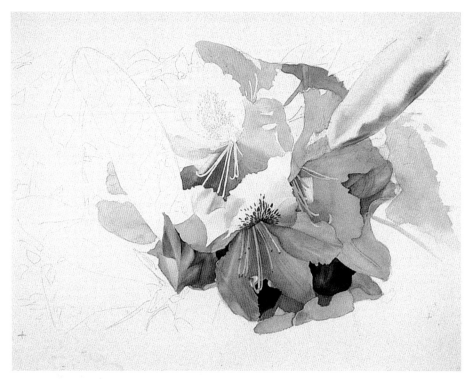

Step 3

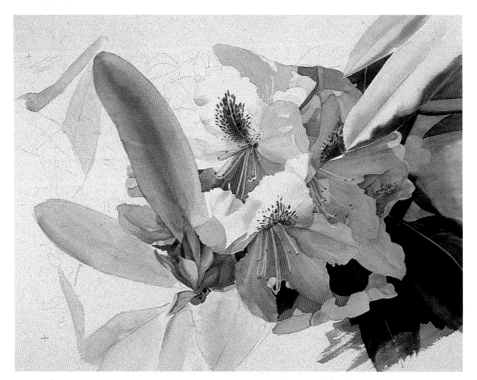

Step 4

3 Creating Leaves

Suggest the presence of a distant blossom with combinations of Cobalt Blue, Alizarin Crimson and Rose Madder Genuine, and let it dry.

The leaves come next. Underpaint the area with a middle-value wash of Cobalt Blue plus a touch of Winsor Blue. Let it dry.

Begin at the right edge of the central leaf, and add New Gamboge to suggest where the sun glances off its side. Immediately add a darker, grayed green. I use Winsor Blue plus a touch of Raw Umber. Paint only up to the edge of the vein. Complete the rest of the leaves in the same manner.

4 Underpaint

You may wonder, why underpaint first? It's because certain greens tend to lift and spread if water is added over them. Therefore, if you want light-value veins, they have to be painted first. Once the paint is dry, add the darker color.

Paint the large backlighted leaf with New Gamboge along the right edge, and add Sap Green as you approach the other side. Let it dry.

5 Paint Dark Shapes

Paint the dark shapes between the veins on the central leaf. Be careful to leave enough of the light underpainting to suggest light coming from behind.

The leaf at the left is in a more or less horizontal position, so the color temperature is cool. Be sure the cast shadow, as well as the leaves in shadow, are dark enough in value.

Once a painting nears completion, it is a good idea to get away, for at least a few minutes, so you can appraise it with a fresh eye.

Can you see how the line of the leaf at the top right (which was intended to point at the central flowers) is beginning to lead the eye out of the composition?

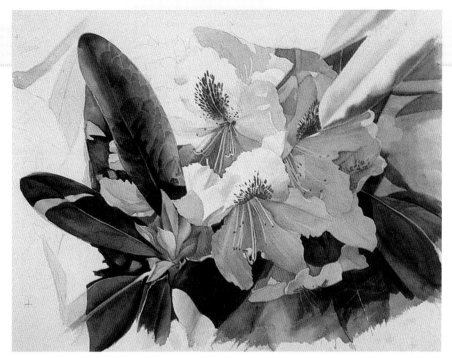

6 Add a Personal Touch

To correct the problem, add another leaf to intersect the offending one. Because the values of the new leaf are darker, it can be added without looking like an afterthought. Finish painting the rest of the leaves.

When you have finished, use your hand to cover the backlighted leaf. With this leaf gone, the painting has become more prosaic, more unimaginative. The simple addition of the leaf presents the subject in a slightly different way. Think of how you can add a personal touch to your next floral.

Step 5

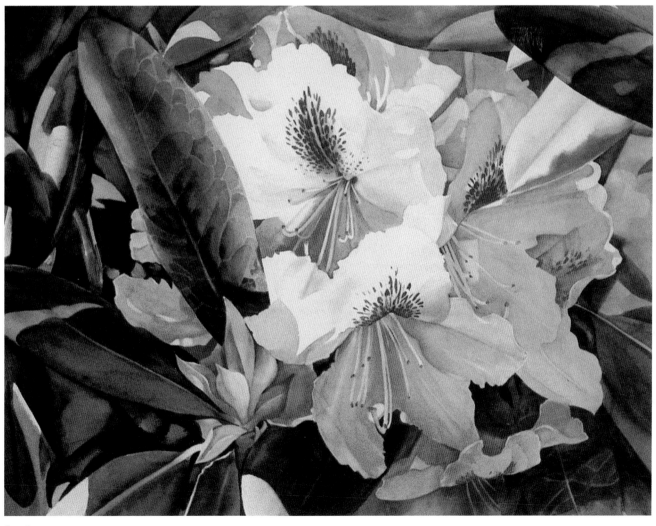

Step 6

Pink Roses

Underpainting for Design Unity

Materials

SURFACE
15" × 22" (38cm × 56cm) stretched
140-lb. (300gsm) Arches cold-press
watercolor paper

WATERCOLORS
Alizarin Crimson, French Ultramarine
Blue, New Gamboge, Red Violet, Rose
Madder Genuine, Winsor Blue

BRUSHES
1½-inch (38mm) flat brush
Nos. 4, 6, 8, 10 and 12 round

Underpainting can help unify a painting as well as create movement and color. All kinds of exciting possibilities may present themselves for lost edges and much more. You really have to try painting this way to understand how much depth and color underpainting can add to your floral.

In this painting, we will be using:
• Curled edges receiving selected light
• Painting convex and concave surfaces
• Cast shadows

Before we paint, let's think about what we want to do with the wet underpainting. Our objective is to create a soft, abstract structure upon which to hang the flowers. To begin, we must leave some white paper where the roses receive the most light. We want to create an organized pattern of dark-and-light shapes along with a pleasing distribution of both warm and cool colors. Finally, our underpainting must be dark enough to remain visible in the finished painting. To be effective, the underpainting value should be between 3 and 5.

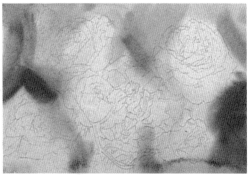

Step 1

1 Painting a Wet-into-Wet Background

First draw the flowers, then using a large brush and clear water, wet the entire surface of the paper (almost to the point of creating a puddle). Use plenty of pigment because the paper is already wet. Add colors one at a time, remembering to leave some areas free of color. If any color should spread into an undesirable area, do not try to pick up or correct at this time. Your only concern should be to create an interesting pattern of warm and cool colors across the page.

2 Painting the Roses

After the surface is completely dry, begin to paint the roses. Use a variety of cool and warm red plus New Gamboge and Red Violet. Study each rose and adjust the color temperature for vertical and horizontal surfaces. The cast shadows are a mixture of Alizarin Crimson, Ultramarine Blue and New Gamboge. Remember, shadows appear coolest at the edge where they meet the light. Keep the overall shape simple, connecting as many shadow shapes as possible.

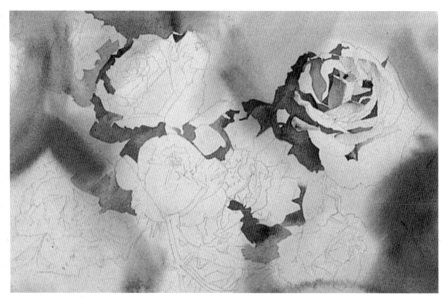

Step 2

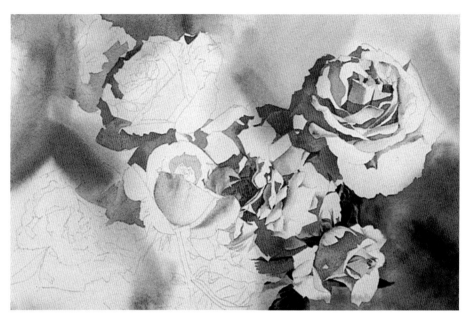

Step 3

3 Adjusting the Background

Work the shadow sides next and be careful to add reflected light wherever possible. Notice how the wet-into-wet underpainting adds structure and color. Once the surface is dry, you may want to re-wet the background in some places to enhance the color or value. Can you see where I darkened the area around the bud on the lower right?

Begin to develop the stems and leaves at the bottom of the page.

4 Final Check

Now is the time to add the final darks and make any corrections. Be sure to check the edges.

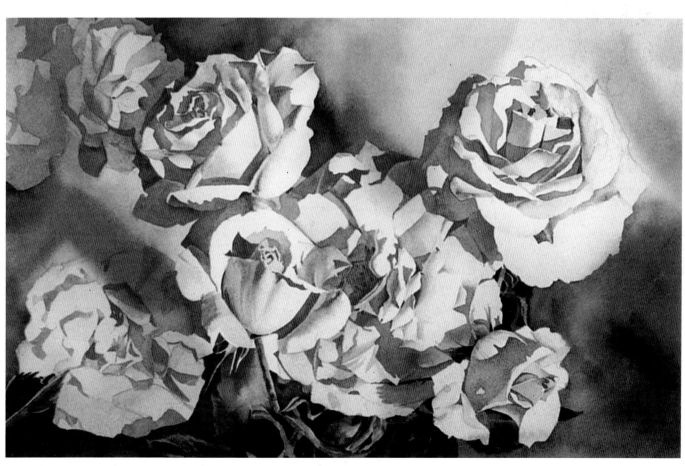

Step 4

Chrysanthemums

Using Contrasting Value, Texture and Color

I have a few pieces of highly prized pre-Columbian pottery given to me by a Costa Rican friend several years ago. The rich brown color and rough surface of the pots contrast nicely with yellow chrysanthemums from the garden.

In this demonstration, I set up a stage. After everything was in place and lighted, I sketched and photographed the final arrangement.

Even though you will find this sketch on page 131, you may want to "eye ball" the drawing, sketching it loosely. The handmade pots have irregular forms, and the flowers are round shapes with little painted detail.

You may want to review the sections in Chapter 8 on:
- "Puddle and pull" brushstrokes
- Painting around complex edges

Materials

SURFACE

15"× 22" (38cm × 56cm) of stretched 140-lb. (300gsm) Arches cold-press watercolor paper

WATERCOLORS

Alizarin Crimson, Brown Madder, Burnt Sienna, New Gamboge, Ultramarine Blue, Red Violet

BRUSHES

1½-inch (38mm) flat

Nos. 4, 6, 8, 12 and 14 round

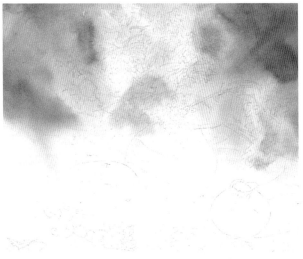

Step 1

1 Setting the Stage

Wet the paper with clear water and underpaint the area behind the flowers with varying mixtures of Brown Madder, New Gamboge, Red Violet and Alizarin Crimson.

2 Adding the Flowers

After the initial wash is dry, use darker values of these same colors to define the edges of the chrysanthemums and stems. Next, add the green leaves with various mixtures of Raw Sienna, Winsor Blue and Cobalt Blue.

Continue painting individual petals, losing edges wherever possible and adding detail. Now and then, stop to determine if there is enough detail to tell the story without overwhelming the eye.

After the paint is dry, carefully re-wet the foreground area with clear water, and add colors, one at a time, permitting them to merge on the paper. Remember, this is a horizontal surface and should be cooler than the vertical surface already painted. Don't worry if you paint over the pots.

3 Developing the Illusion of Sunlight

When the foreground is dry, paint the sunny side of the large bowl. Work wet-into-wet, avoiding the sunstruck spot on the side. I used Alizarin Crimson and Burnt Sienna, adding more Alizarin Crimson to cool the surface as it turns from the light. The top portion of this bowl is a slightly different texture. Suggest this difference with a glaze of Cobalt Blue.

Use these same colors on the small bowl at the right.

Step 2

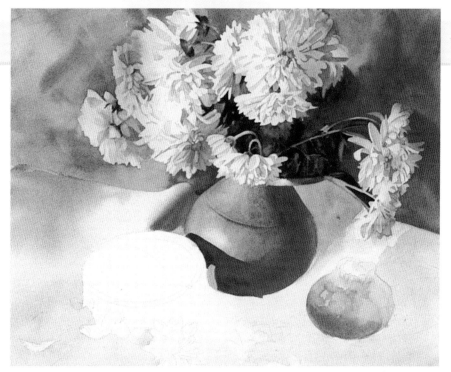

Step 3

4 *Adding Texture and Detail*

The shadow side of the bowls is a dark value, so I blocked in the large shadow shapes first. Paint the bowls in the foreground using the same colors and technique as you did on the large bowl. Glaze the inside of the turtle bowl with Ultramarine Blue to suggest a "used" look. Be sure to keep curved edges soft. Finally, use a stiff, moist brush to lift or correct any highlights.

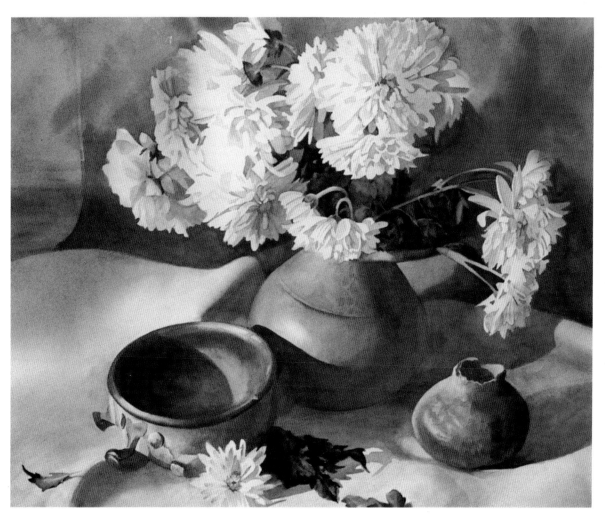

Step 4

Daisies

Painting Reflective Surfaces

This demonstration provides an opportunity to paint several reflective surfaces along with the flowers.

To paint any reflective surface, you may find it best to simply "turn off the left side of your brain" and do as Betty Edwards suggests—just draw and paint what you see. I have described the process on page 110.

Once again, I set up a stage to arrange a setting for the flowers and backdrop.

1 Creating the Mood
Begin with the background. Work wet-into-wet using various blues to create a pattern of color. Leave several white areas for the daisies, but darken the outer corners of the paper to keep the eye within the page.

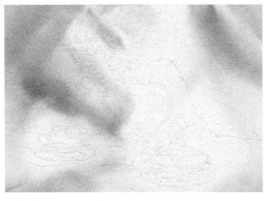

Step 1

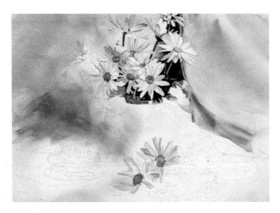

Step 2

Materials

SURFACE
22"× 30" (56cm × 76cm) 140-lb (300gsm) Arches cold-press watercolor paper

WATERCOLORS
Alizarin Crimson, Cobalt Blue, New Gamboge, Raw Sienna, Rose Madder Genuine, Ultramarine Blue, Winsor Blue, Winsor Green, Winsor Red

BRUSHES
1-inch (25mm) flat
Nos. 6, 8, 12 and 16 round

2 Sculpting a Background
As soon as the surface is dry, begin painting the daisies. Darken the color around some petals, letting them appear to emerge from the background.

Next, develop the fold in the background drapery. Wet the area and then add color, letting your brushstrokes follow the direction of the fold.

3 Begin Reflective Surfaces
Underpaint the lightest value of blue on the vase and lid. Add darker shapes as they appear. To paint any reflective surface, think only of the shapes you see, and reproduce them as carefully as possible. Use Raw Sienna, New Gamboge, Burnt Sienna and Rose Madder to suggest the gold color on the cups.

4 Develop Brilliant Surfaces
Begin with the large vase. Paint blue-green on the right side and add a cooler blue toward the center. Use a fully loaded brush, and keep a wet edge as you work across the surface. Paint around the circular

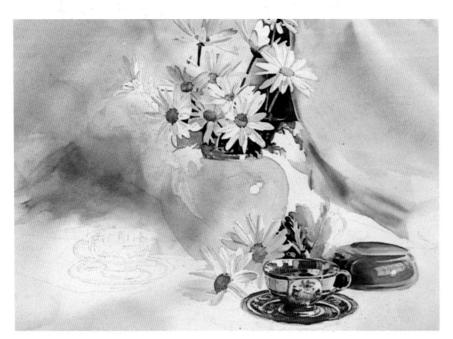

Step 3

highlight and the rectangular reflection. Make sure the brushstrokes follow the contour of the vase. Add darker color as you approach the shadow side.

The cups require a careful look. Examine the color and the shapes you see. Take them one shape at a time and they become manageable.

5 Final Review

Re-wet the background area left of the vase. Use bold brushstrokes of color across the background and into the vase itself. Let the colors merge and be lost in one another.

Now for a final appraisal. If the background drape is demanding too much attention, make it less important with a glaze of Cobalt Blue and Rose Madder. To set the drape back farther still, add leaves to intersect (and break the thrust) of the fold.

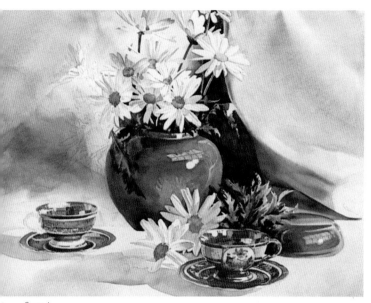

Step 4

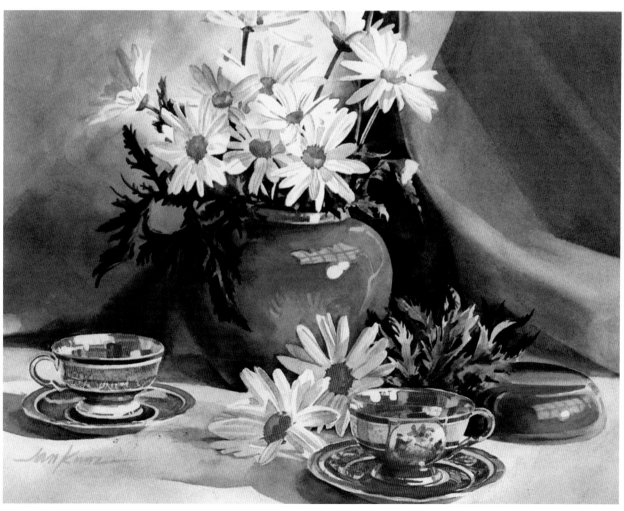

Step 5

Poppies

Discovering Shapes Within the Composition

In this painting, we will draw the principal flowers in position, but not the foliage. The placement, as well as the shapes of the foliage, will be developed from the design opportunities found in the wet-into-wet underpainting.

I know this may sound like voodoo art, but it is possible to see shapes within a wash, especially in a charged wash. This is what we will attempt to do in this painting. You may understand this concept better if you look at the demonstration on pages 88 and 89.

These beautiful poppies make a wonderful subject for a floral painting. They look as if they were make of white crepe paper. I have seen them as large as a salad plate.

Materials

SURFACE
22"× 30" (56cm × 76cm) 140-lb (300gsm) Arches cold-press water-color paper

WATERCOLORS
Alizarin Crimson, Cobalt Blue, New Gamboge, Raw Sienna, Rose Madder Genuine, Ultramarine Blue, Winsor Blue, Winsor Green, Winsor Red

BRUSHES
1-inch (25mm) flat

Nos. 6, 8, 12 and 16 round

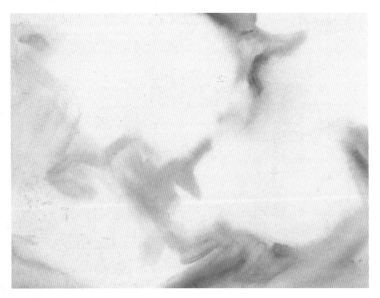

Step 1

1 Getting Started
Wet the entire paper with clear water. Paint warm and cool shapes across the page using considerable pigment on your brush. Try to avoid at least a part of the flower shapes. Your finished wash should be about value 4. Let it dry.

2 Creating Floral Images
Your background will differ from mine. That is as it should be. No two washes are exactly the same.

After the wash dries, begin to paint the flowers by darkening the background colors around them.

Next study your painting and look for subtle shapes within the wash. Go slowly and use your imagination to add stems and leaves as you "find" them. Make the most of the background shapes you have created.

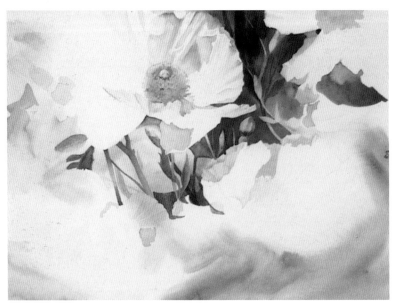

Step 2

3 Thinking Creatively

Continue developing the flower shapes and adding detail. Look for places where you might lose an edge. This is a good way to make the background a part of your painting. Ask yourself if you should glaze back an area, soften an edge or add a stem.

An unforeseen circular shape has developed behind the central blossom in my painting.

4 Checking Edges and Shapes

I use that white shape to suggest another flower. Overlapping shapes help give the illusion of depth. The final step is to survey your work. Are the value relationships consistent? Are the darks dark enough? Use your value scale to check again.

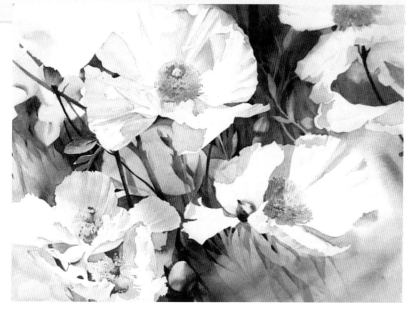

Step 3

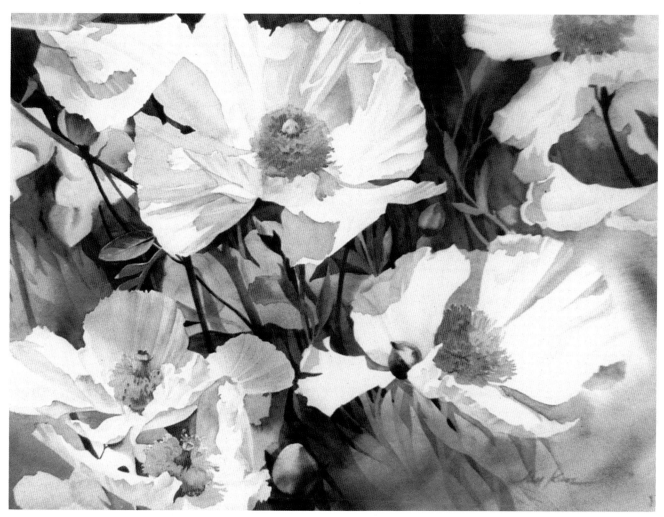

Step 4

Drawings

Since you have read this far, you are no doubt ready to paint a floral masterpiece! At least I hope so!

As promised, here are the drawings I used in the painting demonstrations earlier in this chapter. I have made a grid over them to make it easy for you to enlarge them and paint along with me. If you have not enlarged a gridded sketch before, this is how you do it.

Count the number of squares in the sketch, and draw an equal number of larger squares on your sketch paper. Next, copy the floral drawing, one square at a time. Enlarging a drawing in this manner can make the most complicated sketch manageable.

TOP

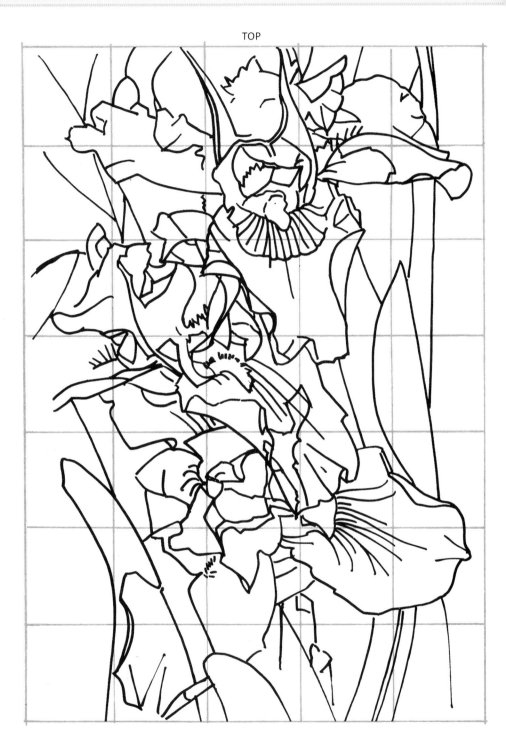

IRIS

This is the drawing for the iris on pages 114-116. I suggest you look at the painting as you draw and include only the lines you want. Some of the shapes are confusing. I was intrigued by the way the swordlike leaf cut through the petal of the bottom iris. The line across the petal is its cast shadow.

TOP

RHODODENDRONS

This painting will give you an opportunity to experiment with various greens. Remember, when you mix complementary colors in dark values, you can get mud. To create a grayed green, I find it best to lay complements next to one another and let them blend on the paper.

TOP

PINK ROSES

I began the painting of the roses on pages 120-121 with a wet-into-wet underpainting. It is a good idea to make the drawing dark enough so the lines will be visible under the wash. If you lose them, they can be reinstated any time during the painting process.

TOP

CHRYSANTHEMUMS

I drew a great deal more information into this painting than I used. The shapes are simple.
The position of the various objects is about all that is needed. Nevertheless, if more drawing
makes you feel comfortable—do it!

TOP

DAISIES

This is the kind of painting I like to start when the house is quiet and there is little chance of interruption. If you are new to painting, I suggest you make the drawing large enough so you can see where you are going. Take your time—you'll do a great job.

TOP

POPPIES

Here is a chance for you to begin with my demonstration painting and add enough of your own creation to make it uniquely your own! Why not start big? You may want to add this painting to your collection.

Reference Photos

Here are a few photographs of flowers that may inspire you to try your hand at floral painting. Feel free to trace over these photos to help yourself get started.

This photo of cosmos would make a better composition if the flower on the lower right were moved a bit to the left.

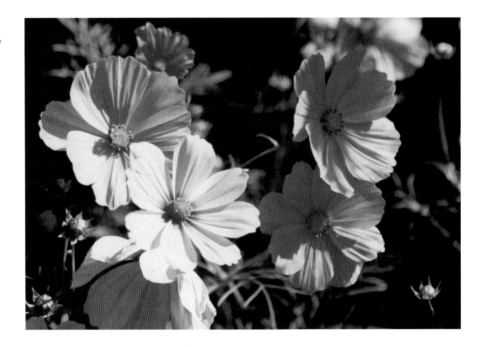

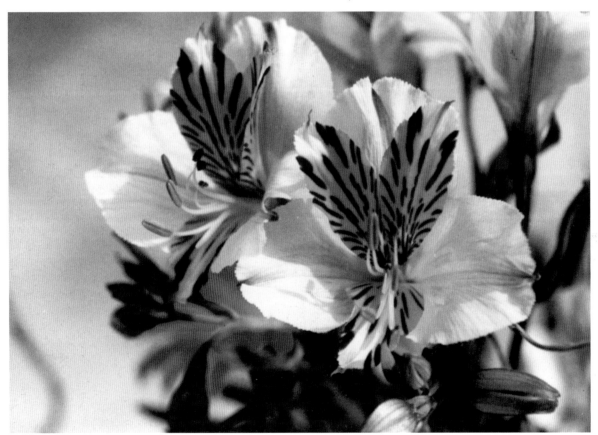

I would begin painting these flowers with an abstract wet-into-wet underpainting.

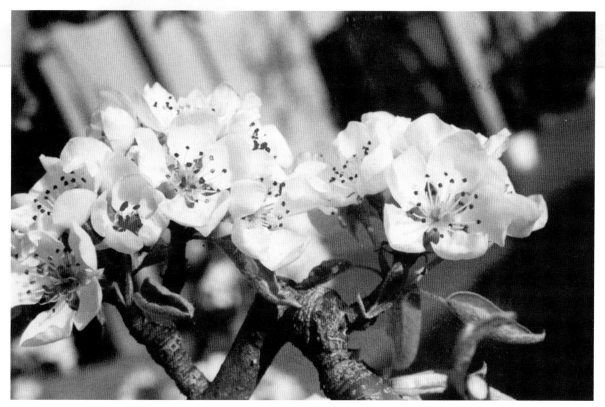

These apple blossoms make a nice path across the page. Watch out for those bold anthers.
Handle them carefully or they could make your painting look spotty!

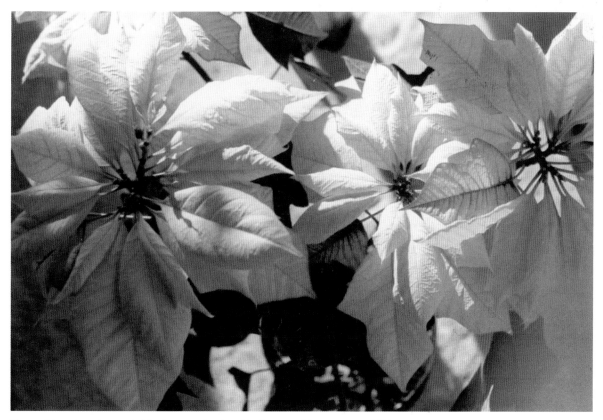

These white poinsettias need a bit of rearranging, but this photograph has great possibilities.

The "One-Two-Threes" of Floral Painting

At the beginning of this book, I suggested that there is no simple "one-two-three" way to paint flowers. However, every floral painting we complete does go through three phases of development. The success of the painting is largely dependent on how much thought we have given to each phase.

PHASE ONE: PLANNING

A. Study the subject.
   Know the subject well enough to be able to draw the blossoms and leaves in any position.
B. Design the picture area.
   Make an S.A.T. sketch, and design the whole picture area. Decide on a vertical or horizontal format.
C. Plan the distribution of color and value.
   A quick color sketch can spotlight potential problems. Use vertical lines to work out a pleasing value plan.

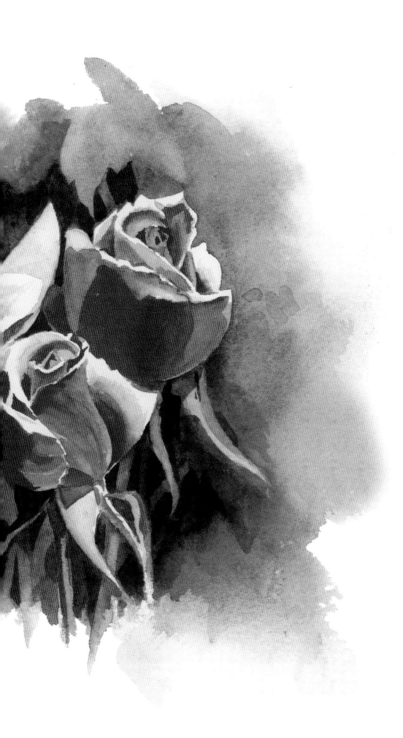

PHASE TWO: DRAWING

A. Make a full-size drawing.
Begin the drawing on tracing paper and use as many overlays as necessary to work out all the bugs.

B. Transfer the final drawing.
Transfer the drawing onto the watercolor paper using the graphite sheet you have made for this purpose.

PHASE THREE: PAINTING

A. Prepare the work space.
Have everything ready before you begin. You will need fresh pigment, clean water and a paint rag positioned where you have immediate access.

B. Decide on a painting method.
This is where you have to feel your way. If there are a great many complicated shapes, you should consider starting on dry paper. Perhaps a wet-into-wet wash is the best way to begin. Go with your instinct.

C. Always take all the time you need.
In the final analysis, we paint with our brains. There is no substitute for thinking! So take your time and enjoy every step of the way.

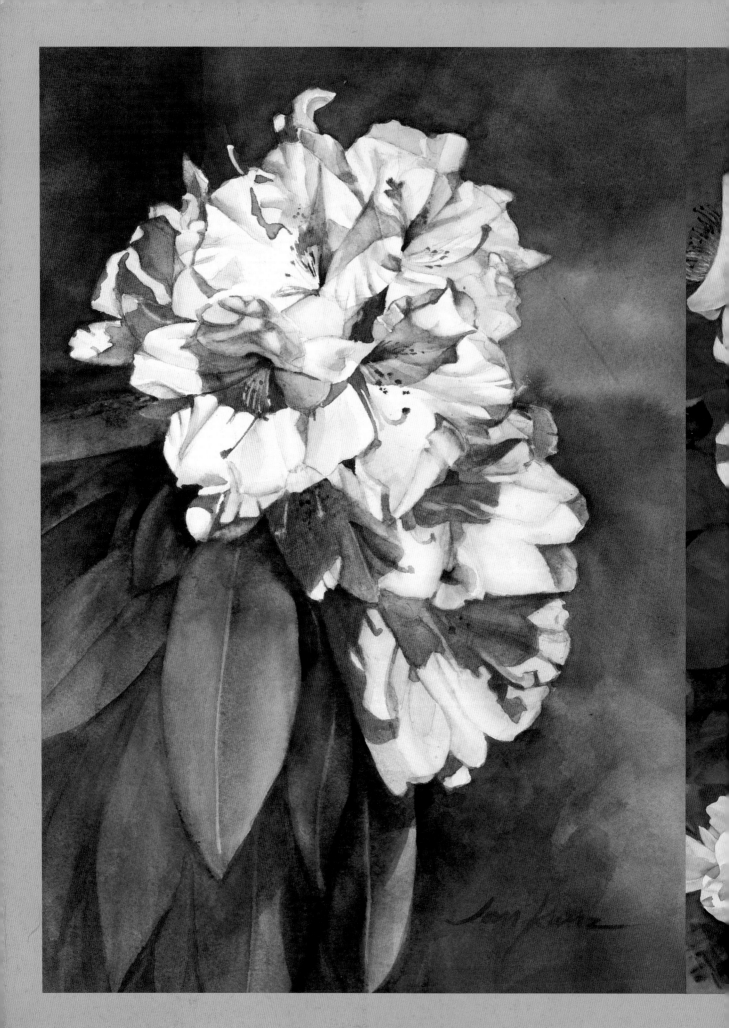

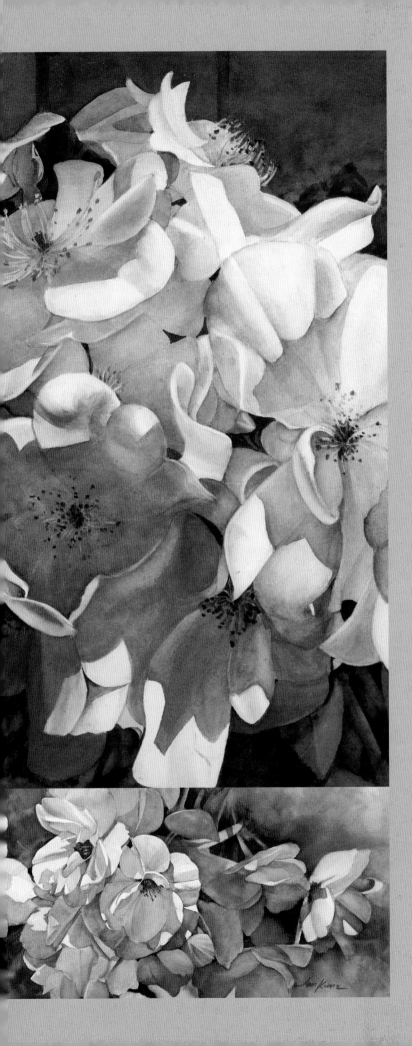

Conclusion

Now and then, even the best of paint-ers will experience times when nothing seems to go right. One artist friend described it as a time when you need to look for your own name in the phone book to see if you are somebody! When this happens, try to be relaxed. It has been my experience that this may be a period of growth and that you will come back better than ever.

One student sent me a photo of her car. The license-plate holder read, "Not afraid of Sap Green." Watercolor paint-ing is full of small victories, but the best reward is always the joy of painting!

Index

Other fine North Light Books are available from your local bookstore, art supply store, online supplier or visit our website at www.fwmedia.com.

15 14 13 12 11   5 4 3 2 1

Distributed in Canada by Fraser Direct
100 Armstrong Avenue
Georgetown, ON, Canada L7G 5S4
Tel: (905) 877-4411

Distributed in the U.K. and Europe by F&W Media International, LTD Brunel House, Forde Close, Newton Abbot, TQ12 4PU, UK
Tel: (+44) 1626 323200, Fax: (+44) 1626 323319
Email: enquiries@fwmedia.com

Distributed in Australia by Capricorn Link
P.O. Box 704, S. Windsor NSW, 2756 Australia
Tel: (02) 4577-3555

Edited by Maija Zummo
Designed by Clare Finney
Production coordinated by Mark Griffin

About the Author

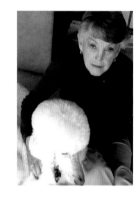

Jan Kunz received her formal education at the University of California. Her interest in commercial and visual arts prompted her to take classes at various art schools in Southern California, where she learned to appreciate the beauty in lettering and graphic design. After retiring from a successful career as a commercial artist and art director, Jan devoted herself to her first love: watercolor painting.

With sketchbook in hand, Jan has traveled widely, documenting people and places from the streets of Alexandria, Egypt to fishermen in Alaska. She has held packed watercolor workshops, and displayed her work in many galleries and shows across the nation. In addition to contributing to numerous books and magazines, Jan has authored five books and four DVD workshops, including North Light's *Painting Beautiful Watercolors from Photographs*, *Painting Watercolor Portraits that Glow*, *Watercolor Basics: Color* and *Jan Kunz Watercolor Techniques*.

Today Jan lives with her dogs, Griff and (camera-shy) Kobe, in their home overlooking San Francisco Bay. Her efforts at retirement have once again failed and her studio door is always open to aspiring artists.

Metric Conversion Chart

To convert	to	multiply by
Inches	Centimeters	2.54
Centimeters	Inches	0.4
Feet	Centimeters	30.5
Centimeters	Feet	0.03
Yards	Meters	0.9
Meters	Yards	1.1

Lilacs and Sterling
30"× 22" (76cm × 56cm)

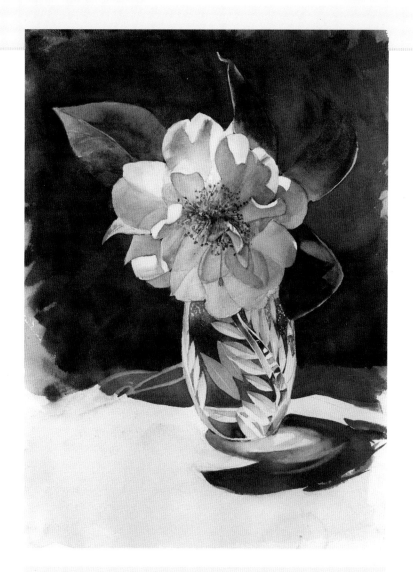

This book is lovingly dedicated to my son Greg,
who has become the rock in my life.

Acknowledgments

Thanks to editor Maija Zummo whose expertise and exceptional
organizational skills have made this a new and better book.
The beautiful appearance of the pages is the thoughtful, handy
work of designer Clare Finney. A special thanks to my daughter
Lynn Powers who is very much in touch with every aspect of the
art community, and to Joan Griffiths who helped with everything from caring for my dogs to proofreading text.

Ideas. Instruction. Inspiration.

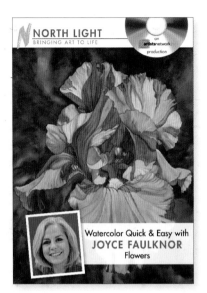

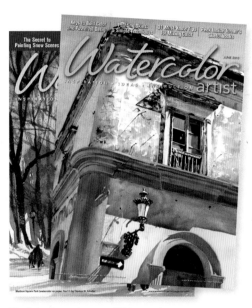

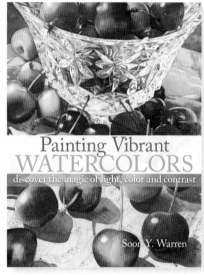

DVD running time: 78 minutes

Find the latest issues of *Watercolor Artist Magazine* on newsstands, or visit www.artistsnetwork.com/magazine..

Hardcover • 144 pages

Receive a FREE downloadable issue of The Artist's Magazine when you sign up for our free newsletter at www.artistsnetwork.com/newsletter_thanks.

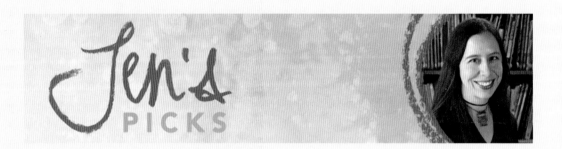

Visit www.artistsnetwork.com and get Jen's North Light Picks!

Get free step-by-step demonstrations along with reviews of the latest books, videos and downloads from Jennifer Lepore, Senior Editor and Online Education Manager at North Light Books.

These and other fine North Light products are available at your favorite art & craft retailer, bookstore or online supplier. Visit our websites at www.artistsnetwork.com and www.artistsnetwork.tv.